WOLVERHAMPTON WANDERERS

MISCELLANY

WOLVERHAMPTON WANDERERS

MISCELLANY

DAVID CLAYTON

AMBERLEY

For a Wolves diehard and a terrific junior coach, Gareth Hughes.

First published 2015

Amberley Publishing
The Hill, Stroud
Gloucestershire, GL5 4EP

www.amberley-books.com

British Library Cataloguing in Publication Data.
A catalogue record for this book is available from the British Library.

ISBN 978 1 4456 4225 3 (print)
ISBN 978 1 4456 4247 5 (ebook)

Typesetting Amberley Publishing.
Printed in the UK.

ACKNOWLEDGEMENTS

Thanks to the countless journalists, programme editors and supporters who committed their thoughts to print over the years and everyone who has played a part in the creation of this book – too many to thank personally – but I thank you all nonetheless.

Thanks to several websites too, including 11v11, Statto.com, Wolves Footy Mad, LTID and Historical Kits, and snippets and quotes from interviews by writers like Henry Winter and many others. Thanks to all the people associated with those websites and newspapers and, again, many thanks to all the unaccredited writers that gave me inspiration during the creation of this book. All reasonable efforts have been made to obtain permission where material has been reproduced from other sources.

There are fantastic mines of information that supporters create online to help researchers and supporters alike, and with that in mind, a massive thanks goes to Gavin Hill and his superb website The Wolves' Site (http://www.thewolvessite.co.uk). Thanks also to the F. C. H. D. for the statistics at the back of the book – the work these guys do is incredible, trust me. I'd also like to thank Wolves writers Tony Matthews, John Hendley and Les Smith (*The A–Z of Wolves* [Breedon Books, 1999] and *Wolves: The Complete Record* [Breedon Books, 1994]) plus David Instone (*Wolverhampton Wanderers Greats* [John Donald Publishers, 1990]).

I've written a number of books on football clubs, but I really enjoyed researching Wolves' history and finding out so much about a team that has contributed so much to English football and produced so many household names over the years. I grew up a Manchester City fan – don't hold that against me – and I recall that Wolves always seemed to leave Maine Road with a decent result. My second ever game was a 2-0 home defeat to Wolves with John Richards scoring both goals. A couple of years later, Wolves won 3-2 at Maine Road so, to my mind, Wolves were a jinx team for City!

Perhaps another affinity with Wolves stems from the fact I was born and raised less than a mile from the venue that the Gold and Blacks won their first FA Cup. My house was half a mile from the Fallowfield athletic track in Manchester where Wolves beat Everton in 1893. In fact, the venue was still around when I was a kid in the early 1980s and I used to regularly go there to have a kick-about on the university football pitch. It had a steep running/bike track around it and that's where the 45,067 fans would have stood as Wolves beat Everton 1-0 all those years ago. It remains the only FA Cup final to have been played on English soil outside London – so I reckon that's not a bad claim! Sadly, the track and field have long since gone, but at least I could say I scored a goal at the same end as Harry Allen, and Harry is the name of my firstborn!

Working for Manchester City as a journalist, I've had the pleasure of visiting Molineux a number of times over the years and it's always been a favourite destination of mine where I never failed to receive the warmest of welcomes from the staff and supporters alike. That's why I'm looking forward to seeing the club back in the Premier League sooner rather than later. I've tried to make this an original and easy read; there's plenty of statistics, facts and tables for easy reference and I know there was another Wolves Miscellany out a few years back, which I purposely avoided reading so as to be as original as possible – I'm sure you'll find both works very different.

Finally, thanks to Tom Furby, Elizabeth Watts and Jenna Whittle at Amberley for giving me the opportunity to write about Wolverhampton Wanderers Football Club, and also to my wife and three kids who I had to sacrifice precious time with as the deadline loomed. I hope you, the reader, enjoy the book and, even if it's saved for those precious quiet few minutes in the smallest room in the house, that's good enough for me.

David Clayton, Manchester, January 2015

WOLVERHAMPTON WANDERERS
MISCELLANY

CHRISTMAS CRACKERS?

Believe it or not, the English League programme used to include playing games on Christmas Day – a fixture that was played up until 1956, though matches on 25 December proved a little hit-and-miss for Wolves over the years.

The first festive game was in 1901 when a trip to Derby County ended in a 3-1 defeat – and things didn't improve much for a while with just five wins from the first 16 attempts. There were some heavy defeats during that period too, including a 5-1 thrashing at Hull City in 1914, a 7-1 loss at Coventry City in 1922 and a 6-2 mullering by Aston Villa in 1933. Oddly, only five of the 25 games played were at home and it was 1933 before Nottingham Forest sent the Molineux hordes home having ruined Christmas! The final Christmas game was a 2-1 defeat at Charlton Athletic – a shame perhaps for a date that had almost averaged four goals per game over the years. The complete record is as follows:

Played: 25
Won: 11
Drawn: 3
Lost: 11
For: 47
Against: 49

BOXING CLEVER

Football on Boxing Day is the perfect antidote to endless TV reruns, turkey leftovers and annoying relatives and will continue to be so, unless the Premier League's whingeing foreign legion eventually get their way and enforce an winter break (God forbid!). But Wolves actually present a very good case for not playing football on 26 December with just two wins from the last 15 played (up to 25 December 2014) – a quite appalling record and the bane of many a Wolves fan, tired of going back to a bedraggled Christmas tree and turkey curry and in a foul mood after yet another loss (which 11 of those 15 have ended up being!). But there have been worse runs than that, with a sequence of 13 Boxing Day games between 1979 and 1995 resulting in no victories whatsoever – eight ended in defeat and five matches were drawn. Looking at the bigger picture, it means Wolves have won just four fixtures on this date in 35 years! No wonder Black Country Christmases have been a little bleaker in recent times. The first Boxing Day match was played in 1899 and ended in a 4-2 Molineux defeat to Blackburn Rovers, and the first 14 Boxing Day games were all played at home and 27 of the first 29 were home fixtures. These days, the Boxing Day game is generally rotated, but the complete record is as follows:

Played: 95
Won: 34
Drawn: 21
Lost: 40
For: 135
Against: 141

FA CUP – THE FIRST TRIUMPH

It didn't take Wolves long to reach their first FA Cup final in March 1893. Having seen off Bolton Wanderers (after a replay), Wolves then saw off Middlesbrough 2-1 at Molineux. A 5-0 third-round win over Darwen was followed by a 2-1 win over Blackburn Rovers in the semi-final – a game played at the Town Ground, Nottingham. The final against Everton was to be played at the recently opened Manchester Athletics Club in Fallowfield, Manchester. In fact, the stadium was a stone's throw away from the patch of ground that would eventually become Maine Road, home of Manchester City FC some 30 years later. With a capacity of 15,000 and 170 police officers on duty, three times the expected crowd turned up and when barriers had been torn down, the throngs made their way into the venue. The majority had no view at all, but the fact they were at the FA Cup final was reward enough for most. Scuffles broke out from time to time, mainly as police tried to maintain some order, but the mood was generally positive and the match began at 3.30 p.m. in warm spring sunshine. Wolves began as underdogs but, fielding an all-English XI, took the game to the Toffees and Dick Topham sent a thunderbolt shot just wide, striking a policeman in the head and knocking his helmet off – it wasn't a good day to be a copper! The only goal of the game came on the hour as Harry Allen tried a speculative long-range effort that deflected past Everton 'keeper Williams to send those from the Black Country in the crowd into raptures. Wolves returned home to celebrate at the Victoria Hotel and the game generated gate receipts of £2,559 – that could probably have been tripled had so many of the crowd simply walked in. For the record, Wolves lined up that day as follows: Rose, Baugh, Swift, Malpass, Allen, Kinsey, Topham, Wykes, Butcher, Wood, Griffin. The gate was officially recorded as 45,067 – a record crowd. As a footnote, a local builder purchased a piece of land at Dudley Road, Wolves' former home ground, and built a number of houses he named the Fallowfield Terrace in honour the club's fantastic achievement.

WOLVES v. OLD BIG 'EAD

Few would argue that Brian Clough was one of the greatest managers ever – but how did Wolves go on against Cloughie? The first meeting against a Clough side was when Bill McGarry's side took on Derby County at Molineux, drawing 1-1. The return game ended in a 2-0 defeat at The Baseball Ground. Though the Rams won 4-2 at Molineux the following season, Wolves won the return 2-1 in Derby, though Clough's side did win a home fourth-round FA Cup tie 2-1. Both teams won their home fixture 2-1 in 1971/72, and in 1972/73 both teams won at the other's home ground – Wolves winning 2-1 in Derby and the Rams triumphing 3-0 in the Black Country. Clough and Peter Taylor resigned in October 1973 and initially took charge of Brighton before embarking on an ill-fated 44 days in charge of Leeds United. Wolves played neither club during that time. In January 1975, Cloughie took over at Nottingham Forest and the first meetings with Clough's new team in 1976/77 ended in a League double for Wolves who won 3-1 at the City Ground and 2-1 at Molineux. In 1977/78, it was Cloughie's turn to celebrate a League double, winning 3-2 at Molineux and 2-0 at the City Ground. Forest won the 1978/79 home clash 3-1, but Wolves won the return 1-0 and the trend continued the following season – both winning at home – as Forest won 3-2 and Wolves 3-1, though Wolves also won the League Cup final 1-0 at Wembley against the Reds. Forest completed the double in 1980/81, winning 4-1 at Molineux and 1-0 in Nottingham. Wolves kept two clean sheets in 1981/82, drawing 0-0 at home and winning 1-0 away, and after a year apart, the teams resumed battle in 1983/84, Clough triumphing 5-0 at the City Ground and Wolves won 1-0 at Molineux – one of only two League wins from mid-January onwards. With Wolves plummeting through the divisions thereafter, there would be only one more clash with a Brian Clough side as the teams were paired in the FA Cup third round at the City Ground – a game edged 1-0 by Forest. Clough retired in 1993 and one of the greatest characters the game had ever seen never crossed swords with Wolves again. So overall, it was nip and tuck with Wolves winning 11 of the 26 matches against Brian Clough teams and losing 13. Interestingly, only two of the 26 games ended in a draw. The overall record is as follows:

Played: 26
Won: 11
Drawn: 2
Lost: 13
For: 29
Against: 41

NEW YEAR'S DAY

Considering the age of the club, there has been relatively little action for Wolves on New Year's Day – just 40 fixtures in fact – which may come as a surprise for those who think a game on this date happens without fail each season. The very first time Wolves played on the first day of the year was in 1890 when Accrington Stanley emerged victors in a 6-3 goal feast. Overall, this is a day Wolves generally do well with only 11 losses from those 40 games and just under half (19) ended in victory. With 10 draws, it seems there is around a 75 per cent chance that Wolves will start the New Year with a positive result.

The 1 January record is as follows:

Played: 40
Won: 19
Drawn: 11
Lost: 10
For: 59
Against: 54

CRAZY HORSE

Liverpool legend Emlyn Hughes joined Wolves after 12 years and 500-plus games at Anfield where he won virtually every trophy available. The broad smile of skipper Hughes, nicknamed 'Crazy Horse', became a familiar sight for football fans during the 1970s, and although he was 32 when he arrived at Molineux, it was still a great piece of business to bring such an experienced player to the club. He made his debut in a 1-0 win over Derby County and would later win the only trophy that had eluded him at Liverpool – the League Cup – when Wolves beat Nottingham Forest 1-0 at Wembley. Hughes continued to play for England for a short while, earning the last of 62 caps in 1980 and he was also awarded the OBE. A popular figure during his two years in gold and black, he made 77 appearances and scored two goals before going on to player/manage Rotherham United in 1981.

THE ROAD TO WEMBLEY #1: THE 1949 FA CUP FINAL

Wolves lifted the FA Cup for the first time in 1949. The journey began at Molineux where a crowd of 46,272 watched the Gold and Blacks thrash lowly Chesterfield 6-0 in the third round. Two goals each for Pye and Smyth plus strikes from Hancocks and Mullen completed the rout, earning a trip to Bramall Lane to face Sheffield United.

Hancocks again was on target – twice on this occasion – plus Dunn found the net as the Blades were beaten 3-0 on their own patch and in front of a crowd just shy of 50,000. Liverpool were the fifth-round opposition as cup fever gripped the Black Country and 54,983 crammed into Molineux to see if Stan Cullis' side could make into the last eight. Liverpool had already earned a 0-0 draw at Wolves earlier in the campaign, but the Merseysiders headed back north having lost 3-1 on this occasion with Dunn, Mullen and Smyth on target.

The draw everyone had dreaded and hoped for in equal measure was next up as Wolves pulled West Brom out of the hat – but Wolves had home advantage for the derby clash and that proved decisive as Mullen struck the only goal of the game to send the majority of the capacity crowd to cloud nine.

Wolves were paired with Manchester United in the semi-final, but the teams couldn't be separated in a 1-1 draw at Hillsborough with Smyth scoring Wolves' goal. The replay at Goodison Park was watched by 72,631 and Smyth scored his fourth of the FA Cup run – that proved enough to send a jubilant Wolves to the final where East Midlands rivals Leicester City awaited.

The Wembley showpiece didn't disappoint. A crowd of 98,920 watched on as Wolves took a 13-minute lead through Pye who headed home a cross from Hancocks, and it was the Gold and Blacks who dominated the first half. Pye bagged a second just before the break to double Wolves' lead.

The Foxes fought back after the break with Griffiths pulling one back on 55 minutes and then only an offside flag prevented an equaliser minutes later. The match was finally settled by Smyth who made it 3-1 and it was Billy Wright who lifted the trophy for the first time.

Wolverhampton Wanderers   3   Leicester City   1
Pye 2, Smyth 1   Griffiths 1

Team: Williams, Pritchard, Springthorne, Crook, Shorthouse, Wright, Hancocks, Dunn, Pye, Smyth, Mullen.
Manager: Stan Cullis
Attendance: 98,920

APRIL FOOLS

The day of practical jokes has not been too kind to Wolves, with just nine wins from 25 attempts over the years. Just two of the first nine April Fool's Day fixtures between 1893 and 1929 ended in victory. Oddly, four of the last ten games on this date have been against Birmingham City, while there have been three games against both Stoke and Manchester City over the years too.

The 1 April record is as follows:

Played: 25
Won: 9
Drawn: 5
Lost: 11
For: 21
Against: 29

THE BLACK COUNTRY DERBY

The Black Country derby is still the fixture both Wolves and Albion fans look for first and it's been going strong for 126 years and counting. These two old rivals have met 149 times, meaning the next encounter will mark a landmark 150th clash. There is no love lost when the gold and black meet the blue-and-white-striped Baggies, with the first meeting on 15 December 1888 ending with a 2-1 Wolves win. In fact, Wolves flew out of the blocks in this fixture, winning the first five and drawing the other with a goals ratio of 15:4. Unfortunately, it couldn't last, and for a time, the results were fairly even; that is, until 27 December 1893 when the Baggies recorded a humiliating 8-0 at Molineux – a dark day indeed! Albion followed that with a 5-1 win at Stoney Lane nine months later. Wolves recorded a 6-1 win at Molineux in 1896 and Wolves won the first derby at The Hawthorns – a 2-1 win in December 1900. West Brom were forced to wait seven years for a win at their new home with Wolves winning two and drawing two of their first four matches there.

On 28 December 1928, Albion's 7-3 home win became the biggest aggregate derby win and, coupled with their 4-2 Molineux win earlier in the campaign, it meant there had been a total of 16 goals scored in the two matches during the 1928/29 season. Those results formed part of a miserable run for Wolves that saw Albion win six and draw two in a run of eight games. On a happier note, between 1952 and 1961, Wolves won eight and drew one of a nine-game run at Molineux before the Baggies won 5-1 in '62. Wolves' response was a 7-0 Molineux win almost exactly a calendar year later – the club's record win to date. Between 1977 and 1980, six of seven meetings ended in a draw. Season 2006/07 saw the most meetings in one campaign – five – plus a first ever FA Cup tie between the clubs. Sadly, the Baggies won four of them, including the cup ties and, agonisingly, both Championship play-off semi-finals: 'twas ever thus…

The first ever meeting in the Premier League was in February 2010 – a 1-1 draw – but the last two top-flight meetings saw Albion win 2-0 at The Hawthorns and 5-1 at Molineux. The total record to date is as follows:

Played: 149
Won: 52
Drawn: 40
Lost: 57
For: 229
Against: 234

(*A full listing of every game between Wolves and Albion appears towards the end of the book.*)

HALLOWEEN HORRORS…

Wolves' record of matches on 31 October is indeed spooky. There have only been 20 occasions when a fixture had fallen on Halloween and Wolves have managed to win just five of them. Wolves have never won an away game on this date, drawing six and losing four of the 10 matches played. Enough to make your blood curdle…

Played: 20
Won: 5
Drawn: 8
Lost: 7
For: 18
Against: 27

CITY SLICKERS

Manchester City may have won the Premier League twice in three years in 2012 and 2014, but there was a time when Wolves were a major bogey team for the Blues. Between 1955 and 1962, Wolves dominated this fixture with some emphatic victories both home and away in a fixture that guaranteed goals for a while. During the 16 matches played during this period, Wolves scored 62 goals – very close to an average of four goals per game – and with City's 29 strikes, it represents 91 goals – 5.6 goals per match! Wolves recorded 8-1, 7-2, 6-4 and 5-1 victories, winning 12 and drawing four. Wolves also won 8-0 in 1933, 7-3 in 1952, and between 1988 and 1999 Wolves won four successive matches at Maine Road. The total goals for this entertaining fixture is 428, a fraction under four goals every time the teams meet – amazing – and Wolves fans will hope history repeats itself at some stage…

The complete record is as follows:

Played: 111
Won: 43
Drawn: 23
Lost: 45
For: 212
Against: 216

CUP WOE

One of Wolves' lowest points of modern times was arguably the three FA Cup first-round ties against Northern Premier League outfit Chorley, when three attempts eventually ended in defeat. The first tie was played at Bolton Wanderers' Burnden Park, which ended in a 1-1 draw. The replay at Molineux also ended 1-1, meaning a second replay at Burnden Park, and this time Chorley – a town where the Chorley cake is far better known than the football team – triumphed 3-0, with Charlie Cooper scoring twice and with Mark Edwards also on target. In 2011, Cooper and the rest of team were reunited at Chorley's Victory Park ground, as the Magpies celebrated the 25th anniversary of that famous night in Lancashire. Former boss Ken Wright said, 'It was an incredible night, and for most of us it was probably the highlight of our careers'. Needless to say, Wolves fans did not mark the occasion.

MORECAMBE, NOT WISE

Wolves have never met Morecambe in League football, but the teams have met twice in the League Cup in recent seasons. The first occasion was in August 2007 and the Lancastrians returned up the M6 with a 3-1 victory. Lightning struck twice when the teams were paired again together in 2013 – this time Ryan Williams' 84th-minute free-kick settled the game in which Morecambe boss Jim Bentley completed a notable double, having been a Morecambe player in the first meeting six years earlier.

QUOTE/UNQUOTE

I'm enjoying how the season's going. But it's not doing any good for my ticker. I was with some friends at Millwall and they said, 'Oh my God, I'd hate to be your heart surgeon', with all my emotions going up and down at these games. It's all enjoyable though.

Chairman Steve Morgan, 2014, after a 3-3 draw with Millwall.

Kenny is a class act. I think everybody connected with Wolves are pleased and proud to have him as part of the club.

Chairman Steve Morgan, 2014.

My abiding memory will be of him charging out of defence at pace and going on the attack. That's pretty rare ... He was strong, he would give you everything. Deano was a determined character. He was a pleasure to work with, a smashing lad. It's so sad.

Don Goodman on the late Dean Richards, 2011.

There will be a few Wolves fans that will be gutted he is joining our biggest rivals but he left a long time ago; he gave his all in a Wolves shirt and it's not like he turned down Wolves to go to West Brom. He loved his time at Wolves and I know for certain he has really fond memories and that he is genuinely overwhelmed by the warmth of the reception he has always received when he has come back with Man City or for testimonials. I know he hopes this does not spoil any of that. He's moving for football reasons and not disrespecting Wolves in any way.

Former 'keeper Matt Murray on Joleon Lescott's move to West Brom, 2014.

LOAD OF BULL #1

Steve Bull broke record after record during the 1987/88 campaign when the Gold-and-Blacks legend was at his prolific best. Bully scored 52 goals in 58 matches and found the net at least once in 33 games that season. He scored four hat-tricks, was on the mark twice on 11 occasions and bagged 34 in 44 League games. He also scored three in the FA Cup, three in the League Cup and 12 in eight Sherpa Van Trophy games, scoring in every round except the final. Strike partner Andy Mutch bagged an impressive 23 goals as well, meaning the double act scored an incredible 75 goals between them in one unforgettable campaign.

SOMETHING IN RESERVE?

Wolverhampton Wanderers second string came into being in earnest during the 1892/93 season where the reserves joined the Birmingham and District League where they would remain until 1921. It was a fine start to life for 'the Stiffs' too, as they won the title having won 15 of their 18 matches, scoring 66 goals and conceding just 12.

WOLF CUBS

Wolves made an instant impression on the FA Youth Cup when it was launched in 1952/53, going all the way to the final where they faced Manchester United over two legs. The Reds all but secured the trophy in the first leg, winning 7-1 in Manchester, though some pride was restored in the return game, which ended 2-2. Incredibly, the two teams would then meet in the final the following season with Wolves scoring 37 goals in just seven games along the way. This time, the final against United was much closer, with the home first leg ending 4-4 but United edging it 1-0 in the return to take the trophy. Just three years later, Wolves lifted the cup for the first time, beating Manchester United in the semi-final before taking on Chelsea. The final proved to be a thrilling battle, with Chelsea winning the first leg 5-1 in front of nearly 20,000 fans at Stamford Bridge but Wolves were far from finished. Despite the deficit, almost 18,000 turned out at Molineux to cheer the lads on and they were rewarded as the youngsters produced a stunning performance. Unbelievably, striker Ted Farmer single-handedly wiped out Chelsea's advantage with just 40 minutes on the clock as he bagged four goals and Cliff Durandt made it 5-0 8 minutes from time, adding another a couple of minutes later. Jimmy Greaves pulled one back shortly after, but Wolves had done enough and the 6-1 margin meant the trophy belonged to Wolves for the first time. It also reaffirmed the club's burgeoning reputation for producing talented young footballers.

In 1961/62, Wolves again reached the final and faced Newcastle United over two legs. The Magpies left the Black Country with a valuable 1-1 draw in the first leg and completed the job in the return, winning 1-0. It was 14 years before Wolves reached the final again and, for the fourth time, the youngsters ended as runners-up in an all-Black Country final against West Brom. The Baggies won 2-0 at Wolves in the first and completed the job in the return with a comprehensive 3-0 victory. 1976 was the last time the club reached the FA Youth Cup final and the club lie 19th in the overall performance table of teams who have either won or at least reached the final. Manchester United, with 10 wins and four losses, easily top the list.

THE ROAD TO WEMBLEY #2:
1960 FA CUP FINAL

Wolves returned to Wembley after an 11-year absence to take on Blackburn Rovers in the 1960 Cup final. Stan Cullis' all-conquering Gold and Blacks began their quest for glory in front of more than 60,000 passionate Geordies. Clamp and Flowers were on target for Wolves in the 2-2 draw that brought the teams back to Molineux and, in another entertaining affair, Wolves won 4-2 with Flowers, Deeley, Horne and Murray all on target.

Charlton Athletic were then dispatched 2-1 at Molineux with Broadbent and Horne on the scoresheet and Cullis' side then travelled to Kenilworth Road in the fifth round, making light work of a Luton Town side who had already lost 5-1 to Wolves in the League. The Hatters were spared a goal on this occasion, losing 4-1 with Mason bagging a brace and Clamp and Murray on target.

A sixth-round tie at Leicester brought back memories of the 1949 final and the Foxes were again beaten – an own goal plus a strike from Broadbent settled the game 2-1, though Leicester would gain revenge a week later in the League as the teams met again, ending a 14-match unbeaten Wolves run in the process. The semi-final proved a test Midlands derby against Aston Villa, played at The Hawthorns, and Norman Deeley's goal was enough to settle the game 1-0. The final against Blackburn was no classic, with disjointed passages of play and hard tackles causing several stoppages. Future Wigan chairman Dave Whelan was stretchered off before half-time with a broken ankle, just moments after Rovers' Mick McGrath had put through his own net. Further goals from Deeley after the break (68 and 88 minutes) ensured the FA Cup would spend the next year in Wolves' already crowded trophy cabinet.

The near 100,000 crowd generated record receipts of almost £50,000 – not quite what a crowd of that size would yield these days!

Wolverhampton Wanderers 3   Blackburn Rovers 0
McGrath 1 (41, o.g.), Deeley 2 (68, 88)

Team: Finlayson, Showell, Harris, Clamp, Slater, Flowers, Stobart, Horne, Murray, Broadbent, Deeley.
Attendance: 98,954

EURO WOE

Wolves' first foray into European competition came during the 1958/59 campaign when Stan Cullis' side faced German champions Schalke 04. A crowd approaching 46,000 saw the clubs draw 2-2 at Molineux, but the Bundesliga side edged the return 2-1 to progress to the next round.

THE REAL DEAL

Wolves fans were treated to a floodlit friendly of the highest calibre when European Cup holders Real Madrid visited the Black Country in 1958, complete with the legendary Alfredo di Stéfano up front. With a massive 55,169 in attendance for the midweek glamour game, the match didn't disappoint. Wolves went ahead through Dennis Wilshaw after just 8 minutes, but Madrid levelled through Marsal. The home fans went wild again just 5 minutes later when Broadbent made no mistake as he converted Jimmy Murray's pass and the prolific Murray made it 3-1 on the hour mark to give the Gold and Blacks the lead, but Madrid finished strongly with Marsal grabbing his second of the game on 80 minutes to set up a tense finish, but Wolves held out for a famous win.

CHELSEA DAGGER

Jimmy Greaves was the scourge of title-chasing Wolves during the 1958/59 season. The future England striker scored five times as the Pensioners beat Wolves 6-2 at Stamford Bridge in front of a crowd of 62,118. Chelsea then came to Molineux and completed the League double with a 2-1 victory, but thankfully it didn't stop the Gold and Blacks and 13 wins from the next 17 games ensured the title came back to the Black Country. It's a funny old game!

ORIGINS

Wolves began life as St Luke's in 1877 when two pupils at St Luke's church school in Blakenhall. The two boys, John Baynton and John Brodie, had been given a football by their headmaster, Harry Barcroft, and decided a football club would benefit the school as well as enable them to use the ball regularly. Little did they know of the enormity of their creation as the fledgling club grew at a rapid pace. After the first ever game on 13 January 1877, St Luke's merged with The Wanderers and in August 1879, Wolverhampton Wanderers were officially born. Two venues were used in the early days before a more permanent home was found at Dudley Road in 1881. Three years later, Wolves won the Wrekin Cup and also played their first ever FA Cup tie as football rapidly became the chosen sport of the working classes. After turning professional in 1888, Wolves were invited to become one of the 12 founder members of the Football League, playing the first ever official game against Aston Villa and finishing the inaugural campaign in a highly creditable third place – not to mention reaching the FA Cup final where Preston North End triumphed 3-0. It was then decided that a grander venue was needed, and in 1889 Wolves moved to Molineux where the club have remained ever since.

MOLINEUX – A BRIEF HISTORY

Wolves' home ground takes its name from successful Black Country merchant Benjamin Molineux. Molineux purchased a tract of land in 1744 and built the grand Molineux House, which later became another business venture in the form of the Molineux Hotel. In 1860, the plot and buildings were bought by a gentleman called O. E. McGregor, who then developed the plot into The Molineux Grounds – a family-friendly pleasure park that had everything from a boating lake to an ice rink and cycling track. Central to all was an area set aside for football, and when Northampton Brewery became the new landlords in 1889, they were happy to rent the grounds off to Wolverhampton

Wanderers. The site was renovated and made fit for football and spectators and, on 7 September 1889, Wolves beat Notts County 2-0 in front of 4,000 fans. In 1923, the club bought the freehold to the land for the princely sum of £5607, and it wasn't long before a new grandstand was constructed on the Waterloo Road side of the pitch. Further stands were gradually added over the next few years, increasing capacity and increasing revenue. It was no surprise when Wolves became the first club to install new £10,000 floodlights in 1953, playing a first floodlit game against South Africa on 30 September 1953 – Wolves won 3-1. As big European teams accepted invitations for floodlit friendlies, game under the lights at Molineux became a regular favourite for supporters in what was then a unique atmosphere. In 1957, a new set of lights – taller, sturdier and brighter – were installed in preparation for Wolves' European Cup games at a cost of £25,000, but the revenue being generated meant it was a wise investment. During the mid to late 1970s, the club began a slow process to update facilities and new stands were built. The stadium also became all-seated due to the Taylor Report in the early 1990s, and today the club boasts one of the best stadiums outside the Premier League with a capacity of 31,700. There are plans to increase the capacity to 36,000 in the near future, although this may depend on the club winning promotion back to the Premier League.

THE TEXACO CUP – A BRIEF HISTORY

Wolverhampton Wanderers fans of an older disposition could be forgiven for smiling as they passed a Texaco petrol station during the 1970s. Wolves entered the competition, which consisted of clubs from England, Northern Ireland, the Republic of Ireland and Scotland that had not qualified for European competitions. It would eventually morph into the Anglo-Scottish Cup from 1975/76 after the withdrawal of Texaco's sponsorship.

Irish and Northern Irish clubs withdrew from the competition after 1971/72 due to political pressure and ongoing troubles in Northern Ireland in particular. The tournament was sponsored by American petroleum giant Texaco to the tune of £100,000 and was instituted to help promote their recent purchase of the Regent filling station chain. Profits around Wolverhampton were about to shoot up dramatically!

Texaco Cup 1970/71

Wolves began their quest for silverware at Dens Park, where 9,892 fans turned out midweek to see Dundee face Bill McGarry's side, who had won just two of their opening nine matches in League and Cup. The Texaco Cup offered an escape from the growing pressure at League level and goals from Bobby Gould and Jim McCallog started the campaign off with a bang.

Although the competition was still more of a curiosity to locals, over 13,000 attended the second leg – a tense affair – when Wolves hung on to claim a 0-0 draw and thus progress 2-1 on aggregate. Next up were Scottish Premier side Morton and a healthy 10,145 turned out at Sinclair Street to see the first leg against Wolves. It would be a disappointing evening for the Greenock faithful as Gould grabbed two goals and Derek Dougan secured a 3-0 win. The return, however, gave some consolation for the Scots as they left Molineux with a surprise 2-1 win in front of 13,821 supporters.

It would be Wolves' away form that was the highlight of the run to the final, with Derry City next up and, again, Gould was on target as McGarry's side secured a 1-0 victory – a third successive win on the road – in front of 10,096 fans. The second leg saw Wolves end their home jinx with a comfortable 4-0 victory over the Londonderry outfit – almost 16,000 fans turned out too. If interest had been minimal in the earlier rounds, the final itself was anything but with Wolves taking on Edinburgh giants Hearts and, following a familiar pattern, Wolves were away for the first leg and two goals from Hugh Curran and another from Mike Bailey gave the visitors a commanding 3-1 first leg lead at Tynecastle, watched by 26,057 fans.

Having secured European football with a 1-0 win over Burnley just two days earlier – and, ironically, elimination from next season's Texaco Cup tournament – a crowd approaching 30,000 turned out to see McGarry's men over the line, but it proved an edgy affair as the Jam Tarts stole the lead but couldn't find the second needed to take the game into extra time. Hearts won 1-0, but Wolves' exploits on the road again proved decisive as the Gold and Blacks won the Texaco Cup 3-2 on aggregate.

Wolves returned to the competition in 1972/73, but interest was already waning. A Molineux gate of 8,734 saw Wolves beat Kilmarnock 5-1 with goals from Dougan (2), John Richards (2) and McCallog. The second leg ended 0-0, but the second-round tie against Ipswich Town ended interest in the competition as the Tractor Boys triumphed 2-1 at Portman Road (Richards, the Wolves scorer) and 1-0 at Molineux. Curiously, those were exactly the same results in the League as McGarry's men ended the season thoroughly sick of the sight of the Suffolk side! For the record, Ipswich went on to beat rivals Norwich City in the final, 4-2 over two legs.

TEN THINGS YOU NEVER KNEW ABOUT KENNY JACKETT...

Kenny was born on 5 January 1962 in Watford.

He only ever played football for Watford, making 428 appearances and scored 34 goals.

In 1983, Jackett his Wales debut in a European Championship qualifier against Norway.

He spent his entire playing career at Watford before his career was ended by injury at the age of 28.

Teams managed: Watford (1996/97), Swansea City (2004–07), Millwall (2007–13).

Jackett earned 31 caps for Wales but failed to score a goal for his country.

After leaving Watford, Jackett spent time as assistant manager to Ian Holloway at QPR and was briefly manager of Manchester City's reserve team.

He won 11 of his 15 games in charge of City's second string.

He took Millwall to the League One play-off final in his first season in charge, losing the final to Scunthorpe United.

Jackett was manager of Swansea City when the club played their last ever game at the Vetch Field.

ROYAL SEAL OF DISAPPROVAL?

Wolverhampton is in the Black Country – but where did the region get its name from? Well, apparently, Queen Victoria supposedly looked out of the window of her train on a journey through the Midlands and saw the smoke and soot-charred roofs and chimneys before uttering the immortal words, 'What a black country this is', before closing the curtains. Cheek!

LEGEND: BILLY WRIGHT

Appearances: 541
Goals: 16

When it comes to Wolverhampton Wanderers' legends, there is no greater name than the legendary Billy Wright. During his incredible career, Wright achieved many notable feats as he served both club and country with distinction, and he did it all with a smile on his face.

Wright showed promise very early on and began life as a striker, scoring ten goals for his school team on one occasion. A local lad, he was an Arsenal supporter as a boy, but when Wolves advertised for local youngsters to come along to Molineux for trials, it would be the beginning of a great journey for the youngster.

It didn't take long for the coaches to spot his potential, and aged only 14, he made his debut for Wolves' B team, having done enough to earn an eight-month trial, but not everything ran smoothly and manager Maj. Frank Buckley informed the teenager he didn't think he had what it took to make the grade. However, the boss had a change of heart and Billy continued to steadily rise through the ranks until he was given his first-team debut against Notts County, but the outbreak of war would interrupt the rookie's progress.

He guested for Leicester City several times during the war before returning to Wolves in 1942 and going on to make more than 100 appearances while the war raged on. By the time it was over, and with Billy now established as a wing-half, he was soon appointed captain, leading his team to glory against Leicester in the 1949 FA Cup final. He then guided Wolves to the second spot in Division One the following season, though it would be another four seasons before he led Wolves to a first top-flight title.

Wright was an inspirational character for a generation of youngsters and was the rock of a team that went on to dominate domestic football in the 1950s – and it wasn't just with Wolves that Wright had become a legend: he was the first England player to win 100 caps as he represented and captained his country over a 13-year period. In fact, he wore the armband for the Three Lions a record 90 times.

He played his final game for the club in 1959 against Leicester City and was awarded the CBE not long after for his services to the game. His career was unblemished, having never been booked once. After retiring as a player, Billy went on to manage his first love, Arsenal, staying in management for four years before moving into television as a pundit and commentator. He wasn't quite finished with Wolves, however, and returned to Molineux as a director in 1990, welcomed with open arms by one and all. Sadly, Billy died four years later aged 70, and his funeral brought much of Wolverhampton to a standstill as people paid their respects to one of the Black Country's favourite sons.

THE ROAD TO WEMBLEY #3:
THE 1974 LEAGUE CUP FINAL

Wolves' third successful Wembley trip saw the Gold and Blacks beat Manchester City in the 1974 League Cup final as Bill McGarry's side won the trophy for the first time.

The journey began at the less than grand surroundings of The Shay, home of Halifax Town, and goals from Sunderland, Richards and Dougan completed a comfortable second-round passage. Lower League opposition were the third-round opponents too, and Tranmere Rovers proved a tricky test for McGarry's men, who were forced to settle for a 1-1 draw courtesy of a Sunderland strike. Wolves won the replay 2-1 (Dougan and Powell on target) and then faced Exeter City who travelled to Molineux for a Wednesday afternoon start that just 7,623 hardy souls managed to attend. Those who did make it were treated to a 5-1 home win courtesy of two goals each for Hibbitt and Richards and another from Dougan. Interest was slightly better for another midweek tie – this time a quarter final against Liverpool – and the 16,242-strong crowd went home happy with Richards' goal enough to book a two-legged semi-final with Norwich City.

The first leg at Carrow Road ended 1-1 – Richards bagging his fifth goal of the competition – and Wolves completed the job at Molineux with more than 32,000 watching Richards do the damage again with the only goal of the game.

With Wolves looking for silverware for the first time in 14 years, Ron Saunders' Manchester City started the game marginally as favourites, and though the teams were only two points apart, City were six places higher than Wolves in the First Division. Both teams went into the game in decent form, with Wolves losing just two of their previous 12 and City had lost just one in eight. The timing of Wolves' goals proved crucial, with Kenny Hibbitt scoring on 44 minutes to break the deadlock, but City fought back with a Colin Bell goal on 58 minutes, making it 1-1. With 5 minutes remaining, John Richards put Wolves back in front – a goal that won the game 2-1 for Wolves and one that sent 30,000 Black Country fans wild.

Wolverhampton Wanderers 2	Manchester City 1
Richards 1, Bell 1	Hibbitt 1

Team: Pierce, Palmer, Parkin, Bailey, Munro, McAlle, Sunderland, Hibbitt, Richards, Dougan, Wagstaffe. Sub: Powell.
Referee: Ed Wallace
Attendance: 97,886

CHARITY BEGINS AT HOME...

The 1954 FA Charity Shield was a special occasion for the Black Country with Wolves and West Brom contesting the 32nd annual curtain-raiser, with the game featuring the winners of the previous season's First Division (Wolves) and FA Cup (Albion). After a season of unparalleled success for the area, Wolves had edged the Baggies by just four points in the end to claim a first ever League title. Albion had gained some consolation in winning their fourth FA Cup, though the fact they'd been denied an historic double still rankled their followers. For the previous 10 years, the League champions got to host the game, which was held during an international break and also meant several players – most notably, Wolves' captain Billy Wright – missed the game as they were on duty with their national sides. In a game full of goals and excitement, Wolves twice held two-goal advantages at 2-0 and 4-2, but were twice pegged back by the visitors who scored twice in a minute each time to peg the hosts back. The game, a thrilling affair watched by more than 45,000, eventually ended 4-4, meaning the Shield was shared for the second time in its history.

Venue: Molineux, Wolverhampton
Date: 29 September 1954
Attendance: 45,035

Wolverhampton Wanderers 4   West Bromwich Albion 4
Swinbourne 2 (12, 62)   Allen 3 (56, 57, 79)
Deeley (46)   Ryan (77)
Hancocks (73)

CELEBRITY WOLVES FANS

From Brooklyn to the Black Country, boxing legend Mike Tyson became a surprise Wolves fan after manager Dean Saunders compared the club's fall from grace to the former heavyweight world champion's slide. Tyson, who hosted a show at Wolverhampton's Civic Hall four years ago, admitted, 'When I'm over in England I would like to see them in action'. Whether that constitutes being a celebrity fan or not is neither here nor there – this is Iron Mike Tyson, star of *The Hangover*, we're talking about!

Edward Elgar, famous for composing 'Land of Hope and Glory', penned the world's first football chant, 'He Banged the Leather for Goal', in 1898. This was in tribute to striker Billy Malpass, apparently, and didn't take off quite as well as 'Land of Hope of Glory'…

Perhaps the Gold and Black's most famous follower is Led Zeppelin's Robert Plant, while Slade's Noddy Holder – 'It's Christ-massssssss!' – is also believed to be a Molineux regular. Monty Python legend Eric Idle is yet another high profile Wanderers fan. (It should have been Wolves fans singing 'Always Look on the Bright Side of Life', not Manchester United!) Singer Beverley Knight and *The Gadget Show*'s Suzi Perry are two more well-known fans.

Club legend Billy Wright is associated with perhaps the first-ever WAG. He married singer Joy Beverley, of the Beverley Sisters, long before David Beckham and Posh Spice made celebrity wives and girlfriends popular in football.

MONKEYING AROUND?

Maj. Frank Buckley, who was manager of Wolves in 1937, injected his players with glands from monkey testicles after trying it out on himself first. Lance Armstrong, eat your heart out. Wolves were widely regarded as the fittest team in the country. You had to have some balls to do that...

PRAWN SANDWICH BRIGADE?

Bill McGarry was an opinionated and, in some ways, progressive manager who had his own views on player diets. Seafood and prawns in particular, for example, were banned because he believed they weakened the stomach and increased the potential for food poisoning. He took a similar view of bread rolls, carefully checking how many were eaten by his players – one being the limit! Legendary striker Derek Dougan said of his former boss, 'McGarry believed that bread slowed you down. He thought it sapped your energy.' Truth is, he was spot on and a little ahead of his time.

THE ROAD TO WEMBLEY #4:
THE 1980 LEAGUE CUP FINAL

Six years had passed since Wolves had beaten Manchester City at Wembley, but John Barnwell's Gold and Blacks were about to start the new decade in the best possible style. The journey to the 1980 League Cup final began with a two-leg second-round tie with Burnley and just 6,103 fans witnessed a 1-1 draw at Turf Moor. Wolves finished the job at Molineux, with Hibbitt and Palmer scoring the goals in a 2-0 win.

Next up were Crystal Palace in a game played at West Ham United's Upton Park and a near-capacity crowd of 30,727 saw Eves and Hibbitt edge a 2-1 Wolves win. Hibbitt was again on target in the fourth-round 1-1 draw at QPR and Carr settled the replay at Molineux with the only goal of the game.

Third Division Grimsby Town proved an altogether tougher obstacle in the quarter-finals, with Wolves happy to leave Blundell Park with a hard-fought 0-0 draw. The expected rout in the replay turned into yet another edgy affair, with the Mariners good value for their 1-1 draw – Gray scoring Wolves' goal. The replay was at Derby's

Baseball Ground and 16,475 finally saw Wolves progress to the final four with a 2-0 victory courtesy of Hibbitt and Richards.

Wolves fans started to feel it might be their year when they were drawn against another third-tier opponent in Swindon Town in the semi-finals, but the Robins won the first leg 2-1 (Daniel for Wolves), leaving Wolves an uphill task in the second leg at Molineux. More than 41,000 crammed in to see the game and Wolves did just enough, running out 3-1 winners to secure a place at Wembley against Brian Clough's all-conquering Nottingham Forest who were the League Cup and European Cup holders at the time.

With a crowd of 96,527 generating receipts of £625,000, Wolves, led by former Liverpool legend Emlyn Hughes, were resolute in defence and managed to frustrate Forest's free-flowing football. In the 67th minute, a long punt up-field by Daniel led to confusion in the Forest box between Shilton and a defender and the ball bounced loose for Andy Gray to tap home what proved to be the winning goal and a second League Cup triumph for Wolves.

Wolverhampton Wanderers 1   Nottingham Forest 0
Gray 1

Team: Bradshaw, Palmer, Parkin, Daniel, Hughes, Berry, Hibbitt, Carr, Gray, Richards, Eves. Sub: Colin Brazier.
Referee: D. Richardson
Attendance: 96,527

ROLL CALL – WOLVES HONOURS IN BRIEF...

League: First Division
Champions: 1953/54, 1957/58, 1958/59
Runners-up: 1937/38, 1938/39, 1949/50, 1954/55, 1959/60

Second Division/Championship
Champions: 1931/32, 1976/77, 2008/09
Runners-up: 1966/67, 1982/83
Play-off winners: 2003

Third Division/League One
Champions: 1923/24 (North), 1988/89, 2013/14

Fourth Division
Champions: 1987/88

Cups
UEFA Cup:
Runners-up: 1972
FA Cup:
Winners: 1893, 1908, 1949, 1960
Runners-up: 1889, 1896, 1921, 1939
Football League Cup:
Winners: 1974, 1980
FA Charity Shield:
Winners: 1949*, 1954*, 1959, 1960* (* joint holders)
Runners-up: 1958
Football League Trophy:
Winners: 1988
Texaco Cup:
Winners: 1971

TESTIMONIALS

There have been numerous farewell games involving Wolves players over the years. Here is a selection of the most memorable matches…

Billy Wright and Jimmy Mullen: 30 April 1962
Wolves *v.* International XI
A slightly disappointing gate of 14,466 turned out to pay their respects to two Wolves icons. Tom Finney was among those who took part on the day with Ted Farmer scoring a hat-trick for Wolves, with Jimmy Murray notching the other. Typically, Albion's Derek Kevan hit a hat-trick as the teams shared eight goals in a 4-4 draw.

Peter Broadbent: 17 March 1965
Wolves Past & Present XI *v.* International XI
With 13 goals scored between the two teams, this was an entertaining spectacle for those who turned out (a figure was never officially announced). Wolves lost 8-5 with Broadbent scoring twice and Nat Lofthouse and Ronnie Allen guested for the Gold and Blacks.

Ron Flowers: 12 October 1970
Wolves *v.* International XI
Another high-scoring affair – as testimonials sometimes are – Wolves beat the International XI 8-4 in front of a healthy 21,021 Molineux fans. Gordon Banks was in goal for the International XI and he was in fine company with Jimmy Greaves and Bobby Moore completing a notable trio of World Cup stars.

Dave Woodfield: 30 April 1974
Wolves *v.* International XI
It was a time when opposition fans were less likely to attend than those who wanted to see some of the biggest names of the day. Indeed, Elton John turned out for Wolves and another rock god, Robert Plant, also turned out in gold and black, though Rod Stewart was a no-show. A crowd of 14,625 turned out on Woodfield's big night, which featured several different matches. Gordon Banks, Mike Pejic, Tony Brown, Alistair Robertson, Colin Stein, Geoff Hurst, Duncan McKenzie, Frank Worthington, Asa Hartford and Ian Hutchison were also playing in a 5-2 win for the International XI, with the attendance perhaps boosted by Wolves' recent League Cup triumph over Manchester City.

Dave Wagstaffe: 6 May 1975
Wolves *v.* International XI
Yet another Wolves versus an International XI and yet another gate around the 14,000-mark – 13,901 to be exact – for crowd favourite Dave Wagstaffe. John Richards scored Wolves' only goal and Trevor Francis bagged the winner for the International XI, who triumphed 2-1. The game raised around £8,000 for Waggy.

Derek Dougan: 20 October 1975
Wolves XI *v.* Don Revie XI
At last – a variation on the theme as Wolves took on a Don Revie XI – but since when did a testimonial finish 0-0? Typical, seeing as The Doog bagged so many goals during his Wolves career, but a clue to how competitive this game was perhaps. A huge 25,658 turned out for a real Wolves cult hero who, at 37, had decided to finally hang his boots up. An interesting game saw the Revie side captained by Gerry Francis, along with future Wolves players Alan Dodd and Dave Thomas.

Mike Bailey: 20 October 1976
Wolves *v.* Albion

As testimonial committees realised opposition fans could swell the coffers, at last, a local derby! George Best turned out for Wolves, perhaps fulfilling a lifelong dream (!), and a crowd of almost 20,000 (19,733) reflected a big appetite for the game for the locals – as well as a desire to pay tribute to Bailey who had been a popular figure during his long association with the Gold and Blacks. Bailey made around £11,500 with the home support delighted by two Best specials and another from Willie Carr in a comprehensive 3-0 win that also saw the great Bobby Moore become an honorary Wolves player for the evening.

THE WIT AND WISDOM OF DEAN SAUNDERS

Dean Saunders quickly became a cult figure in football for his bizarre press conference quotes. Here is a selection of the best – or should that be the weirdest – ones during his brief spell as Wolves boss…

And another thing that has pleased me is Ladbrokes: we're not one of the three favourites to get relegated and they don't normally get it wrong. They have looked at our squad and thought 'they will get out of it' and that's what I'm thinking.

Saunders, February 2013, highlighting that Ladbrokes do indeed get it wrong sometimes.

I've never been sacked before and I will not be sacked here.

Saunders tempts fate yet again at his inaugural press conference as Wolves boss, six months before he was sacked.

We've got players here with the knack. You always have an eye for a goal but you can lose your eye of the tiger. I've still got my eye for goal now but if you lose your eye of the tiger you are not actually moving to where the ball is going. It is belief and confidence. When you are scoring, you have got the eye of the tiger.

Saunders goes all Katy Perry on us – what on earth was he on about?

At the same press conference, by which time Wolves fans were wondering what they were about to receive, God help us:

> I have got self-belief. If you said to me 'Do you want to open the batting for England? They are playing down the road', I'd say 'Go on then, give me a bat'. Then I'd get to the bottom step and see the fast bowler marking his run-up and realise I can't do that. But my first reaction is 'I will give it a go'.

And there's more – loads of them:

> When your wife serves you up something unhealthy for tea you need to tell her to make something different.

> When the baby is up crying in the middle of the night, you need to tell your wife to go deal with it because you can't play football when you're tired and it's the football that pays for all her expensive things like putting the kids through school.

> If you have no personal pride and you don't really care how you play on a Saturday, you will stop and have a cheeseburger and chips when you feel like one. But if you've got pride that you won't play well if you eat it, you don't eat it. And you won't stop by the pub and drink three pints of lager if you're worried about how you're going to play in four days' time; you go home.

> We might have to risk him, and if his hamstring goes, he's got all summer to get over it.

> It's only Burnley and Brighton, it's not as if we're playing Arsenal and Man United.

> We won't have a particular way of playing. We'll change it up from week to week. The opposition won't know what's hit them!

MOLINEUX INTERNATIONALS

England have played four internationals at Molineux over the years, the first being in 1891, long before Wembley Stadium had even been thought of. England thrashed Ireland 6-1 on 7 March that year in front of 15,231 fans.

It would be 11 years before the national team returned, and on 14 February 1902, Ireland were again put to the sword, losing 4-0 in front of a crowd of 24,240.

The first loss at Wolves came 34 years later when England were beaten 2-1 by Wales in front of a crowd of 22,613.

The final full England international played at Molineux was on 5 December 1956 when England comprehensively beat Denmark 5-2.

WE'VE WON THE LOT!

At last, an unprecedented, best-ever tag that nobody can take away from the club: the Gold and Blacks have won every division they've played in, including the Second (1931/32), the Third (1989), the Fourth (1988) and even the old Third Division North (1923/24). Several teams, including Nottingham Forest, Derby and Blackburn, have won three out of the four, but it is Huddersfield Town who have come the closest to matching Wolves' achievement, with only the Third Division title just eluding them (they finished third twice in 1983 and 1992). Eat that Chelsea, United, Liverpool and City!

THE A TO Z OF WOLVERHAMPTON WANDERERS

A – Abandoned

On the face of it, seeing a game abandoned through heavy snow is not the best, particularly when you are 2-0 up against the Albion! But that's what happened on Boxing Day 1962 when Wolves fans headed for the exits after the teams failed to appear for the second half. The good news is the rearranged game, three months later, went even better, with Wolves running riot against our Black Country cousins with a 7-0 win.

B – Barcelona

Yes, Wolves have faced the great and good and once took on the mighty Barcelona in the European Cup no less. OK, the Catalans didn't have Lionel Messi or Luis Suarez among their number, but a crowd of

80,000 watched the first leg in the Nou Camp with Barcalona winning 4-0. The Spaniards were a huge draw in the second leg with more than 55,535 packing into Molineux to see the La Liga side triumph 5-2.

C – Carl Zeiss Jena

Wolves encountered East German side Carl Zeiss Jena on the way to the 1972 UEFA Cup final. On a snowy pitch in Jena, John Richards scored the only goal of the first leg and Wolves eased through after a 3-0 second leg home win.

D – Durham City

Wolves met – and beat – Durham City twice during the 1923/24 Third Division North season. The matches were played on Christmas Day and New Year's Day and Harry Lees scored twice in each game – a 2-1 win at Molineux and a 3-0 win at Durham.

E – European Football

Wolves' first competitive European game was against German side Schalke 04 on 12 November 1954. In front of almost 48,000, the match ended in a 2-2 draw, with Peter Broadbent scoring both goals and becoming the first player to find the net in a European competition.

F – Five-a-Side

Wolves were the undisputed five-a-side kings of the mid-1970s, winning a national competition in 1976 and 1977. The first final saw Wolves beat Spurs and, a year later, Stoke City suffered the same fate.

G – Grounds

Wolves' first home ground was at Windmill Field, where the club played their games between 1877 and 1879, and the capacity was around 2,000. Then it was John Harper's Field until 1881 when Dudley Road became the new home of the fledgling Black Country club. It was at Dudley Road that the club played their first FA Cup tie and Football League game, and Wolves stayed there for eight years until Molineux became their permanent residence in 1889.

H – Hat-tricks

Although Steve Bull's 18 trebles for Wolves is unlikely to be beaten anytime soon, the first hat-trick was scored by Harry Wood against Derby in 1889. Another notable treble was John Richards' hat-trick against Charlton in 1976 – not bad seeing as he started as a sub!

I – Ipswich Town

Wolves didn't meet Ipswich Town competitively until 1961/62 when both teams won their home game: that's a long wait considering both teams had been in existence for many years.

J – Juventus

Wolves met the Turin giants in the 1971/72 UEFA Cup, with a precious 1-1 draw secured in Italy and a 2-1 win at Molineux seeing Wolves into the semi-finals.

K – Kendall, Mark

Mark Kendall joined Wolves from Newport County in 1986 and he was the Club's No. 1 during the meteoric rise back up the leagues. In 1987, he set a club record of 28 clean sheets in one season and clocked up a total of 177 appearances before joining Swansea in 1990.

L – Leeds City

Rather than powerful neighbours Leeds United, Wolves met Leeds City on 20 occasions between 1906 and 1919, winning eight, drawing four and losing eight. Wolves twice won 5-0 at home and recorded another 5-1 win at Molineux as well. After Wolves' 4-2 win in October 1919, Leeds City were forced to disband and their fixtures were taken over by Port Vale.

M – Mascot

Choosing a mascot for Wolves has never been hard – it's always been a wolf! In the early 1990s, 'Wolfie' became a regular fixture at Molineux and became quite a character, mixing it up with Albion's Baggie Bird and, comically, causing mayhem with Bristol City's Piglets! There was one unsavoury clash between Baggie Bird and Wolfie that ended with an FA enquiry. Well, he's a wolf – what do people expect?

N – New Brighton

There were just two League games played between Wolves and Merseysiders New Brighton. The matches took place during the 1923/24 campaign and both ended in Wolves wins – 5-1 at Molineux and 1-0 in New Brighton. In 1901, Wolves also thrashed New Brighton 5-1 in the FA Cup, meaning it probably wasn't the club's favourite fixture.

O – Overseas

Wolves' first official foreign tour was in 1931 when the team travelled to France for an international tournament. Spaniards Santander won the first game 3-1 and First Vienna beat Wolves 4-2 in Paris to complete an interesting but ultimately miserable trip.

P – PSV

After winning the 1980 League Cup, Wolves met PSV Eindhoven in the European Cup Winners' Cup in the first round of the competition. Unfortunately, PSV won the first leg 3-1 and though Wolves valiantly battled back in the Molineux return, the 1-0 score line was not enough to save elimination.

Q – Queen

Queen Elizabeth II visited Molineux twice. The first time Her Majesty stopped by was to inspect the soldiers of the North and South Staffordshire Regiments and present them with their colours in front of more than 30,000 people. The second occasion was 1988 when Her Majesty opened the newly designed Molineux in front of 2,000 people.

R – Rangers

Wolves have only met Rangers competitively on two occasions, both during the 1960/61 European Cup Winners' Cup semi-final.

On 29 March, almost 80,000 crammed into Ibrox to roar the
Scots home 2-0 and, with one foot in the final, Rangers completed
the job in the second leg, drawing 1-1 in front of a crowd
of 45,163.

S – Shop

The first official club shop was opened at the North Bank End of
Molineux in 1968. Selling an array of hats, scarves, mugs, slippers
and various other paraphernalia, it initially did a roaring trade.

T – Taylor, Jack OBE

One of the greatest referees of the 1970s, Jack Taylor was universally
respected throughout the game. The Wolverhampton-born official
was in charge of the 1974 World Cup final and wasn't afraid to make
the big calls, awarding the Dutch a first-minute penalty. Following
his retirement from the game, he became Wolves' commercial
manager from 1978 to 1982.

U – USA

Wolves have enjoyed several tours of the United States, the first
of which began in May 1963 and, during a lengthy ten-game tour,
Wolves remained unbeaten and bagged 38 goals along the way, with
Ted Farmer returning home with 11 goals. In 1967 Wolves entered a
tournament in Los Angeles and played as the 'Los Angeles Wolves'.
Wolves reached the final and beat Aberdeen 6-5 in front of almost
18,000 fans at the LA Coliseum.

V – Venus, Mark

The wonderfully named Mark Venus undoubtedly had one of the
most memorable surnames in football. He turned professional in
May 1985 with Hartlepool before moving to Leicester. He left Filbert
Street for Molineux in March 1988 and went on to play 337 times in
gold and black, scoring 10 goals.

W – Weather

The first game of the 1906/07 season saw Wolves take on Hull in temperatures that topped 90 degrees Fahrenheit. The teams laboured in the heat, drawing 1-1 in front of an estimated 6,000 Molineux fans.

X, Y – Youth Cup

Wolves and Chelsea contested the 1958 FA Youth Cup final and it was the Black Country boys who triumphed 7-6 over two legs. This was after Wolves had lost successive finals in 1953 and 1954 to Manchester United and there was further heartbreak against Newcastle United in 1962 and West Brom in 1976.

Z – Zenith Data Systems

This annual ill-fated competition took place between 1989 and 1992, with Wolves entering on all four occasions. The first time saw Sheffield United win 1-0 at Bramall Lane, then after beating Leicester City 1-0 at Filbert Street in 1990, Leeds United won 2-1 at Molineux to end interest (what little there was). The final tie was played in 1991 when Grimsby Town secured a 1-0 win at Blundell Park.

KEANE AS MUSTARD?

Profile: Robbie Keane (1997–99)
Appearances: 87
Goals: 29

While nobody doubts Robbie Keane would have eventually become a Wolves legend had he stayed long enough, few expected the talented Irish youngster to stay at Molineux for too long.

Born in Tallaght in Ireland, he began life with local side Crumlin United. He soon attracted the attention of a number of top English clubs including Liverpool and Wolves. It was the Black Country rather than Merseyside that the teenager headed for, believing he could force his way into Wolves' first team quicker. This was a theory that proved correct when he made his senior debut aged only 17 years 32 days old, scoring twice on a memorable debut. Keane went from strength to strength and the 1998/99 campaign saw the youngster grab 16 goals to finish top scorer, confirming his reputation as one of the country's hottest properties. He won the first of his record haul of international caps in 1998 – it was 138 and counting in early 2015 – as he began a path that would set a plethora of new records for Ireland. Wolves initially resisted the temptation to cash in, but when Coventry City tabled an offer of £6 million, Keane left for the Sky Blues on a deal that was a British record for a teenager at the time. He later played for Inter Milan, Leeds United, Liverpool, Spurs, West Ham, Celtic, Aston Villa and LA Galaxy during a distinguished career that was still active in the MSL in 2015. The total transfer fees for Keane during his numerous moves total in the region of £75 million – a huge amount of money. A good pub quiz line on Robbie is that he is a second cousin (once removed) of former melancholic lead singer of The Smiths, Morrissey.

CLUB LEGEND: DEREK DOUGAN

1966–75
Appearances: 307 (+16 sub.)
Goals: 123

As characters go, 'The Doog' is up there with the best of them. The colourful striker led the line with great aplomb for almost a decade in gold and black. A huge crowd favourite, Dougan was born in Belfast in January 1938 and after starting out in the Irish League he joined Portsmouth in 1957 where he switched from defender to forward. His first goal, ironically, was against Wolves in November 1957. He moved to Blackburn in 1959 and played in the 1960 FA Cup final against Wolves, though ended on the losing side as his future employers triumphed 3-0 at Wembley. After 25 goals in 59 appearances, he was signed by Aston Villa boss Joe Mercer for £15,000. Dougan had a similar record to Blackburn at Villa Park – 26 goals in 50 games – before he was on the move again, this time to Peterborough United in 1963 for £21,000. A familiar pattern was emerging as the Dougan moved on again two years later – the fourth time he'd moved on after two years – to Leicester City, where he did his customary two-year stint and, as ever, averaging a goal every other game before moving to Wolves for £50,000 in March 1967 – a transfer he later claimed was the 'best move of his career'. He announced his arrival at Molineux in style, grabbing a hat-trick against Hull City, and ended top scorer in three out of the first five seasons in gold and black before calling time on his Wolves career in 1975. He became player boss at Kettering between 1975 and 1977 and thereafter hung his boots and retired from the game completely. Sadly, The Doog passed away in 2007 aged 69 – just two years after he'd been a pall-bearer at George Best's funeral. He kept a high profile after leaving the game, appearing on TV panels for games and, on one occasion, *Question Time*, with viewers enjoying his outspoken views. He also wrote several books and was chairman of the PFA from 1970–78. In 1982, he was part of a consortium that rescued Wolves from liquidation and became club chairman for three years. The Doog is still remembered by Wolves fans affectionately and his legacy, apart from an excellent record of games and goals, is his long-standing record of being the club's top scorer in Europe with 12 goals; he is the only Wolves player to score a hat-trick in a European competition. There was only one Doog!

SIXES AND SEVENS

Wolves' record friendly victory is a whopping 19-1 away win to Manchester East End in 1888. Harry Wood bagged six of the goals and Jack Brodie bagged seven on a memorable afternoon in the Rainy City.

LOAD OF BULL #2

Quotes By or About Club Legend Steve Bull…

I don't want to leave Wolves. The crowd love me. I love them. What do I want to leave that behind for?

Steve Bull, shortly after winning his first England cap.

Steve was totally dedicated with a great attitude. But circumstances were that I had to sell him. I was looking for players to take Albion into the First Division. He wasn't good enough for that then. I had to make a decision because Albion needed the money quickly.

Ron Saunders on his decision to sell Steve Bull to Wolves.

We had a bond – an instinctive thing. I never felt Andy got enough credit. He scored over 100 goals here but could have had more if he hadn't been so unselfish.

Bully on strike partner Andy Mutch.

There was a raw aggression, determination and strength about his play, and, of course, this ability to put the ball in the back of the net. He could create chance for himself and finish the odd one off. We tried to get him but Ron [Saunders] wouldn't let him go. In the meantime, we had picked up on Andy Thompson and tried to do a deal for him instead. This was a few weeks later, but the day before, I decided to have one last go for Bull. Just on the off chance. Ron this time agreed to do business.

Graham Turner on his best piece of managerial business.

We were third bottom in the Fourth Division and facing a replay against Chorley in the FA Cup. Me and Andy Thompson were ineligible. We lost 3-0 and the pair of us sat in the bar, having a pint and eating sausage rolls, asking each other, 'What have we done?'

Bully, shortly after walking into the lions' den.

It was strange being thrown in among top-class players like Gascoigne, Barnes and Waddle. I was nervous to start with, but once I'd had a couple of training sessions they brought more and more out of me. Lineker was the boss's blue-eyed boy at the World Cup in 1990. Him and Peter Beardsley were at the top of their game so I can't complain. If I'd come on the scene later, when Lineker was fading out, I might have had more of a run. I felt I did myself justice, but I wish I'd had as many games as someone like Ian Wright.

Bully on his all too brief England career.

I was very close to going. I'd already sorted everything out with Coventry City manager Ron Atkinson when I rang my wife to ask what she thought. She said, 'Whatever you decide, we'll support you.' I just said, 'Oh sod it, I've been here nine years – why move?' No disrespect to Coventry, but if it had been Villa, Liverpool or Man United it might've been different. They're not as big a club as Wolves.

Bully on why his proposed transfer to the Sky Blues never happened.

I've only got a 10-mile drive from home and travelling up and down motorways isn't for me. Why unsettle a rock if it's happy where it is?

Bully on why he stayed loyal to the Gold and Blacks.

The most influential manager? Ron Saunders. None of this would have been possible if he hadn't got shot of me.

Bully on his favourite manager.

Any with my left foot – I normally use it just for standing on.

Bully on his 'greatest' goal.

PLAYER OF THE YEAR

The club's official Player of the Year award has been active since 1967. Here is a list of winners since 2000:

Year	Winner
2000	Ludovic Pollet
2001	Lee Naylor
2002	Alex Rae
2003	Joleon Lescott
2004	Henri Camara
2005	Joleon Lescott
2006	Kenny Miller
2007	Matt Murray
2008	Wayne Hennessey
2009	Kevin Foley
2010	Jody Craddock
2011	Matt Jarvis
2012	Wayne Hennessey
2013	Bakary Sako
2014	Kevin McDonald

RECORDS, HONOURS AND ACHIEVEMENTS

Player Records

Appearances

	Name	Years	Lg	FAC	LC	Other	Total
1	Derek Parkin	1968–82	501	46	35	27	609
2	Kenny Hibbitt	1968–84	466	47	36	25	574
3	Steve Bull	1986–99	474	20	33	34	561
4	Billy Wright	1939–59	490	48	0	3	541
5	Ron Flowers	1952–67	467	31	0	14	512
6	John McAlle	1967–81	406	44	27	31	508
7	Peter Broadbent	1951–65	452	31	0	14	497
8	Geoff Palmer	1971–84	416	38	33	8	495
9=	Jimmy Mullen	1937–60	445	38	0	3	486
9=	John Richards	1969–83	385	44	33	24	486

(*Source: Wikipedia*)

Individual Player Feats

Appearances

Most League appearances: 501 – Derek Parkin (1968–82)

Most FA Cup appearances: 48 – Harry Wood (1887–98) and Billy Wright (1939–59)

Most League Cup appearances: 36 – Kenny Hibbitt (1968–84)

Most European appearances: 18 – Derek Dougan (1967–75)

Most consecutive appearances: 171 (127 League) – Phil Parkes (September 1970 – September 1973)

Oldest player: Archie Goodall, 41 years 116 days (*v.* Everton, Division One, 2 December 1905)

Highest Goalscorers

	Name	Years	Lg	FAC	LC	Europe	Other	Total
1	Steve Bull	1986–99	250	7	18	0	31	306
2	John Richards	1969–83	144	24	18	4	4	194
3	Billy Hartill	1928–35	162	8	0	0	0	170
4	Johnny Hancocks	1946–57	157	8	0	0	2	167
5	Jimmy Murray	1955–63	155	7	0	2	2	166
6	Peter Broadbent	1951–65	127	10	0	7	1	145
7	Harry Wood	1887–98	110	16	0	0	0	126
8	Dennis Westcott	1937–48	105	19	0	0	0	124
9	Derek Dougan	1967–75	95	4	7	12	5	123
10	Roy Swinbourne	1945–57	107	5	0	0	2	114

(*Source: Wikipedia*)

Most goals in one season in all competitions: 52 – Steve Bull (1987–88, Division Four)

Most League goals in a season: 38 – Dennis Westcott (1946–47, Division One)

Most top-flight goals scored: 158 – Johnny Hancocks (1946–57)

Most goals in European competition: 12 – Derek Dougan (1967–75)

Most hat-tricks scored: 18 – Steve Bull (1986–99)

Most goals scored in a match: 5

> Joe Butcher *v.* Accrington, 19 November 1892 (Division One)
> Tom Phillipson *v.* Bradford City, 25 December 1926 (Division Two)
> Billy Hartill *v.* Notts County, 12 October 1929 (Division Two)
> Billy Hartill *v.* Aston Villa, 3 September 1934 (Division One)

Fastest Recorded Goal

It took just 18 seconds for John Richards to find the net as Wolves took on Burnley at Turf Moor in November 1975. The prolific

Richards, who had scored three goals in his previous two games against the Clarets, added another in a 5-1 win in Lancashire and just for good measure, Richards bagged another brace in a 3-2 win at Molineux later in the season to make it seven goals in four games against Burnley. Lessons learned, the Clarets held the Gold and Blacks to a 0-0 draw for the opening game of the 1976/77 campaign – though it's worth noting Richards didn't play for Wolves!

International Milestones

Wolves' first international cap was won by Charlie Mason for England against Ireland on 17 March 1884. Mason played for Wolves between 1883 and 1892 and made 108 appearances, scoring twice. The most international caps won while playing for Wolves will probably take a long time to be beaten, with Billy Wright accumulating 105 caps for England between 1939 and 1959. The most international goals scored while a Wolves player is ten; Ron Flowers and Dennis Wilshaw both holding the record (both while representing England). The most World Cup finals appearances accolade again goes to Billy Wright, who played ten matches at the tournament finals between 1950 and 1957.

Player Award Winners

The most notable non-club player award was the prestigious Football Writers' Footballer of the Year 1952 honour that was bestowed on Billy Wright. The Wolves legend bagged the honour at the end of the 1951/52 campaign and as an indication of the calibre of players who this accolade was awarded to by the nation's journalists, the next two winners were Nat Lofthouse and Tom Finney.

Transfer Records/Milestones

It's always interesting to look at the timeline of a club's transfers, and Wolves' is no different.

From 1963 to the present day, the fees have (obviously) grown with inflation. The present record held for a transfer fee paid is the £6.5 million Wolves agreed with Reading for the services of Kevin Doyle in June 2009 and the same fee was paid to Burnley for Steven

Fletcher in June 2010. The highest fee received is £14 million from Sunderland for Steven Fletcher in August 2012.

Progression of Record Fees Paid

Date	Player	Bought from	Fee
September 1963	Ray Crawford	Ipswich Town	£55,000
February 1968	Derek Parkin	Huddersfield Town	£80,000
July 1972	Steve Kindon	Burnley	£100,000
September 1977	Paul Bradshaw	Blackburn Rovers	£150,000
September 1979	Andy Gray	Aston Villa	£1.469 million
March 1995	Dean Richards	Bradford City	£1.85 million
September 1999	Ade Akinbiyi	Bristol City	£3.5 million
June 2009	Kevin Doyle	Reading	£6.5 million
June 2010	Steven Fletcher	Burnley	£6.5 million

(*Source: Wikipedia*)

THE SUBWAY ARMY

Wolves used to have a notorious hooligan gang known as 'The Subway Army' during the 1970s and early 1980s. The gang earned its name due to the fact they would attack rival fans as they passed through the subway next to Molineux. Like many hooligan elements of the era, they were eventually dissolved by specialist police and intelligence units including Operation GROWTH – the latter standing for Get Rid of Wolverhampton's Troublesome Hooligans.

THE LIQUIDATOR

Popular reggae classic 'The Liquidator' was a familiar tune played before home games for a good number of years at Molineux. The song, recorded in 1969 by the Harry J. All-stars, was adopted by a number of clubs including Chelsea, St Johnstone, Wycombe, West Brom and Northampton Town, who all claimed they were the first to play the tune as a sort of club anthem, but it's almost impossible to say who really played it first. What is true is that West Midlands Police requested Wolves stop using the tune as it promoted abusive chanting and hooliganism. For the record, the offensive words were 'fuck off West Brom', in case you were wondering. Despite this claim – or perhaps because of it – the song remains popular with the majority of Wolves fans.

10 QUICK-FIRE WOLVES FACTS TO IMPRESS YOUR MATES IN THE PUB

You ask: When were Wolves formed and how did they do in that first season?
Answer: Wolves became founder members of the Football League in 1888, finishing third in that inaugural season as well as reaching the FA Cup final, losing 3-0 to Preston North End.

You ask: Who is Wolves' record appearances holder?
Answer: Derek Parkin has made the most appearances – 609 between 1968 and 1982.

You ask: What is Molinuex's record attendance?
Answer: The highest attendance recorded for Wolves was 61,315 recorded against Liverpool in the FA Cup fourth round on 11 February 1939 – offer a bonus point for the score – a 4-1 win for Wolves.

You ask: Including every League game ever played (since 1888), where do Wolves sit in the all-time League table?
Answer: Wolves are fourth overall, behind only Manchester United, Liverpool and Arsenal.

You ask: Who has scored the most goals for Wolves? – and there's a bonus point for the number of hat-tricks within that total (a gimme!)
Answer: Steve Bull, with 306 goals from 1986 to 1999. Bull scored an incredible 18 hat-tricks.

You ask: True or false? Wolves were the first club to score 8,000 League goals.
Answer: False – Wolves were the first club to score to 7,000 League goals; they achieved this when Seol Ki-Hyeon scored in the 1-1 draw at Crystal Palace on 10 December 2006.

You ask: Who is the club's record scorer for a single game? Steve Bull or Joe Butcher?
Answer: Joe Butcher – he scored five against Accrington in 1892.

You ask: How many major trophies have Wolves won?
Answer: Wolves are the eighth most successful club, behind Chelsea, with 13 major trophy wins.

You ask: What unique record to Wolves hold in England?
Answer: Wolves remain the only club to have won all top national domestic titles and cups – the FA Cup (1893, 1908, 1949, 1960), the Football League Cup (1974 and 1980), and Football League Trophy in 1988 as well as all four divisional titles.

WHAT DO YOU GET FOR THIRD, THEN?

Here's a question to put your mates on the spot – what do Manchester United, Stoke City, Birmingham City, Wolverhampton Wanderers and Burnley have in common?

The answer is that they've all finished third in the FA Cup. Yes, third! Between 1970 and 1974, the FA introduced an annual match between the losing FA Cup semi-finalists to replace the traditional match between England and Young England. The matches were played at a neutral venue but – shock horror – the experiment's unpopularity was reflected in poor attendances and the idea was binned after five years. Incidentally, the 1972 game between Stoke and Birmingham finished goalless with Blues winning 4-3 on penalties – notable for no other reason than it was the first ever FA Cup game to be decided via a penalty shoot-out. Wolves appeared in the 1973/74 play-off – played three months after the FA Cup final – and beat Arsenal 3-1 at Highbury with 21,038 fans bothering to watch. McCallog and Dougan (2) were on target.

SUPER SUB

Wolves legend Jimmy Mullen holds two landmark records for England. Jimmy became England's first substitute when he came on for Jackie Milburn of Newcastle United in a 4-1 victory against Belgium in Brussels on 18 May 1950. The International Football Association Board had authorised substitutions by advance agreement between opponents in friendly matches in 1932, but substitutions in international play generally were not approved until the 1970 World Cup. Mullen was also the first sub to score for England when he found the net in the same game against the Belgians.

THE ANGLO-ITALIAN CUP

Wolves' first foray into the Anglo-Italian Cup came in 1969 when the Gold and Blacks took part in the 1969/70 post-season tournament. The format was an unusual one to say the least. There were six English teams: Swindon Town, Sheffield Wednesday, Middlesbrough, West Bromwich Albion, Sunderland and Wolves plus six Italian teams: Napoli, Juventus, Roma, Fiorentina, Lazio and Vicenza. The teams were split into three groups consisting of two English and two Italian teams each, and each team played against the two teams in their group from the opposing nation (stay with us). Matches were played home and away with the first legs played in England and the second legs played in Italy. Two points were awarded for a win, one point for a draw, and a point for each goal scored (got all that?).The team with the highest number of points from each nation then contested the final and Wolves were mightily unlucky not to reach a money-spinning final.

Bill McGarry's side beat Fiorentina 2-1 at Molineux (Dougan and Wagstaffe scored) before another home win followed with a 1-0 win over Lazio (Bailey). A 3-1 win over Fiorentina in Florence put Wolves in the box-seat for a place in the final, but failure to score in the 2-0 defeat in Rome to Lazio – watched by 43,073 fans – meant Swindon pipped Wolves to the inaugural final. Played in Naples against Napoli, Swindon won 2-0 in front of a crowd of 55,000.

Wolves entered the competition again in 1992/93, losing 2-1 to Tranmere Rovers before beating Peterborough United 2-0 – but it was the Wirral side who progressed, having also drawn their other game. The table finished thus:

	Pl	W	D	L	F	A	Pt
Tranmere Rovers	2	1	1	0	2	1	3
Wolverhampton W	2	1	0	1	3	2	2
Peterborough Utd	2	0	1	1	0	2	1

Wolves had a couple more stabs at the competition in 1994/95, but again, failed to get past the group stages after a 3-3 draw with Stoke City and a 2-2 draw with Birmingham City:

	Pl	W	D	L	F	A	Pt
Stoke City	2	1	1	0	5	3	4
Wolverhampton W	2	0	2	0	5	5	2
Birmingham City	2	0	1	1	2	4	1

The final attempt for Anglo-Italian glory was in 1994/95. The preliminary English groups were scrapped after poor attendances and instead, the competition started with the international stage. Wolves beat Lecce 1-0 in Italy but went down 1-0 to Ascoli at Molineux. A 2-1 loss to Venezia meant the 1-1 home draw with Atalanta was largely academic and Notts County and Stoke progressed from the English sector, with Ascoli and Ancona the Italian group toppers. Notts County beat Stoke in the semis and then Ascoli 2-1 in the final at Wembley. The group results were as follows:

International Stage

Group A
Ascoli 1-1 Notts County
Lecce 0-1 Wolverhampton Wanderers
Swindon Town 0-2 Atalanta
Tranmere Rovers 2-2 Venezia
Atalanta 2-0 Tranmere Rovers
Notts County 1-0 Lecce
Venezia 1-0 Swindon Town
Wolverhampton Wanderers 0-1 Ascoli
Tranmere Rovers 0-1 Ascoli
Atalanta 1-1 Notts County
Swindon Town 3-1 Lecce
Venezia 2-1 Wolverhampton Wanderers
Notts County 3-3 Venezia
Wolverhampton Wanderers 1-1 Atalanta
Lecce 0-0 Tranmere Rovers
Ascoli 3-1 Swindon Town

Italian Table

	Pl	W	D	L	F	A	Pt
Ascoli	4	3	1	0	6	2	10
Atalanta	4	2	2	0	6	2	8
Venezia	4	2	2	0	8	6	8
Lecce	4	0	1	3	1	5	1

English Table

	Pl	W	D	L	F	A	Pt
Notts County	4	1	3	0	6	5	6
Wolverhampton W	4	1	1	2	3	4	4
Swindon Town	4	1	0	3	4	7	3
Tranmere Rovers	4	0	2	2	2	5	2

SUPER MICK MCCARTHY QUOTES

Born: 7 February 1959 in Barnsley
Playing career: Barnsley, Manchester City, Celtic, Lyon, Millwall
Managerial career: Millwall (1992–96), Republic of Ireland
(1996–2002), Sunderland (2003–06), Wolves (July 2006–February
2012) Ipswich Town (November 2012–present)

No genuine Wolves fan has a bad word to say about former boss
Mick McCarthy, with his pearls of wisdom, forthrightness and
plain old Yorkshire grit. Here are some Mick facts and some of
his best quotes:

> At the moment we've got 16 players. The MM on my tracksuit stands
> for Mick McCarthy – not Merlin the Magician.

August 2006 news conference before his first game as Wolves boss.

> I disrespected the Premier League? No, I didn't. I paid it the biggest
> compliment I could because I made a decision driven completely
> by one thing: the desire to stay in it. That is the only issue for me,
> just as it is the only issue for about another 10 managers. And every
> one of them knows why I did what I did. The Burnley result was
> paramount, I know that. It could have gone tits up from there but,

instead, we're on 19 points and not in the bottom three. Before, everyone was laughing at us. Another promoted team that couldn't cut it in the Premier League. Some cheeky sod wrote that Liverpool had Wolves coming up on Boxing Day, so that was three points guaranteed. And those same people then criticise me for managing our season the way I think is best? Do me a favour. I called it a career-defining moment but all big decisions are like that. When Sir Alex Ferguson changed his goalkeeper halfway through an FA Cup final was it career defining? Of course it was. Same with Rafa at half-time in the Champions League final.

Look, I don't like hypothetical questions, but here's one. Say it is the last game of the season and we need three points to stay up. We've got Manchester United away on the Wednesday, Burnley at home on the last day. Two draws is no good for us. What team do you pick at Old Trafford? What team would the fans want you to pick? So would I do it again? Yes.

Mick bites back for fielding a weakened team against Manchester United, December 2009.

I've had a lovely letter from Tiger thanking me for taking the pressure off him. Apparently he's driving round in his car singing 'Super Mick McCarthy'.

December 2009 (after fielding a weakened team against Man United at Old Trafford, shortly after Tiger Woods' fall from grace).

Alistair McGowan is the only one who does me better than me. I've heard him. He is quality.

Mick is relaxed after someone used a fake Twitter account in his name.

Yes – but that's easy for me to say. The reality is I don't know. We'd stayed up for one or two seasons prior to that and been in worse positions. And I do think I'd have kept the club up.

Mick responds to questions whether he would have kept Wolves up the season he was shown the door.

Opinions are like backsides. We've all got them, but it's not wise to air them in public.

> September 2011 (response to QPR captain Joey Barton's
> Twitter taunts).

I thought I had seen it all when it comes to the fickleness of football folk. Then I heard Spurs fans singing 'There's only one Alan Sugar'.

> Mick after a trip to White Hart Lane.

Stuart Pearce's thoughts on Mick:

I like the fact he is so even-handed. He was probably the only manager that when I used to watch matches I would turn the radio on for. I always put the local station on as I left town just to listen to his interviews so I could have a chuckle down the M5! That tells you something. He played for the Republic of Ireland when I played for England in 1990 and we also faced each other at club level. But I'm cut from a different cloth; he's cut from granite – that's the difference.

General Snippets

Carl Robinson has got a busted hooter and Daz Carter has got blurred vision. They were having a chat and thought they were in the crowd.

I was feeling as sick as the proverbial donkey.

Anyone who uses the word 'quintessentially' in a half-time talk is talking crap.

I think one or two of our legs got a bit leg weary.

No regrets. None at all. My only regret is that we went out on penalties. That's my only regret. But no, no regrets.

The other day in training he wanted to join in an eleven-a-side game and I had to say, 'Kyler, no!', and he went away and kicked three or four balls all over the pitch. Then he was made to go and fetch them because he'd thrown his toys out of the pram.

Mick on Kevin Kyle's (unsuccessful) attempt to rush back from injury.

Every single one of the players has been slapped around the head but they keep coming back for more.

Fucking abysmal, that was what I fucking thought of it. C'mon, let's get to it, I'm trying my best here. What did I make of it? I thought it was the best bit of fucking football I've seen in a long time. Do me a favour. It was a crap start to a game. There you have it, can you print all that? Fucking rubbish, absolute tosh. Drivel. Shite. Bullshit. That's what I thought of it. Did that help? I'm quite pleased, apart from the fact that's given them the poxy result, I'm fucking livid about it – of course I am. So, there you have it.

Mick reacts to an own goal scored against Reading in 2009 after just 60 seconds.

We've got the drug testers here today. They shouldn't be going to see the players. They should go to see the officials instead.

Reporter: No yellow cards today?
McCarthy: No and I asked all the lads to go out there and knock seven bells out of everybody as well like I normally do. Shame that isn't it? They went out there and played free-flowing football and were rampant for 45 minutes. What were they playing at?

What I learned from Jack [Charlton] – ensure that you're all inside the tent pissing out and get rid of any fellow who's outside the tent pissing in.

Before the goal it was two rubbish teams playing rubbish football.

The Serbian 'keeper is a big tart doing that [going down injured] because there's nothing wrong with him.

I started [trying to give up alcohol] on Shrove Tuesday and then by Ash Wednesday something had happened and I'd had a bottle of beer.

I'd rather be favourites for Premiership relegation than favourites to win the play-offs.

And finally...

To prove Mick has lost none of his wit, after a 1-1 draw with Leeds in January 2014 as Ipswich Town boss, he said, 'Some people might be frustrated with that result? Some people can fuck off.'

Thanks for everything, Mick!

COSTLY GOAL!

In these days of highly paid players and goal bonuses, it's hard to imagine scoring a crucial goal and it actually leaving you out of pocket – but that's exactly what happened when Peter Knowles scored a vital winner for Wolves away to Portsmouth in February 1967. Knowles' header secured a 3-2 win for the visitors and in a moment of celebration, Knowles booted the ball over the stand and out of Fratton Park. Unimpressed, Pompey officials then sent Knowles a bill for around £7.50 when the ball was declared missing after a brief search of the area at the back of the stand. The bill was settled in Knowles' name, but it's hard to imagine the club itself didn't foot the bill.

CROWD PULLERS

Four of Molineux's top five attendances have come in the FA Cup and, with the current capacity as it is and no sign of a stadium expansion anytime soon, it seems unlikely these records will be broken for many years – if at all. Interestingly, the four FA Cup records came during the boom time for the competition during the 1930s when club records were set up and down the land. Wolves fans flocked to see their team like never before. The four records were set consecutively over a period of two years starting in 1937 when the February FA Cup fourth round clash with Grimsby Town attracted 56,799 people. The first game at Blundell Park had ended 1-1, but Wolves triumphed 6-2 in the replay. The fifth round tie with Sunderland bettered that crowd by just under 1,000 as 57,751 saw Wolves held 1-1 by Sunderland. The teams drew at Roker Park before the Black Cats won a second replay 4-0 at Hillsborough. A year later, the fourth round tie against Arsenal saw 61,267 fans crammed into Molineux to see the Gunners triumph 2-1 and, just over a year later, Wembley-bound Wolves beat Liverpool 4-1 in front of a record crowd of 61,315. However, with war breaking out later that year, it spelled the end of the boom years for the competition. The biggest League crowd on record was recorded 10 years later on 15 October 1949, as 56,661 fans watched the Black Country Derby against West Brom end in a 1-1 draw. The lowest crowd on record was the October 1891 clash with Notts County that attracted just 900 hardy souls to see Wolves win 2-1.

For the record, the box office games' top is as follows:

Attendance	Date	Opponents	Competition	Rounds
61,315	11 February 1939	Liverpool	FA Cup	5
61,267	22 January 1938	Arsenal	FA Cup	4
57,751	6 March 1937	Sunderland	FA Cup	5
56,799	24 February 1937	Grimsby Town	FA Cup	4
56,661	15 October 1949	WBA	Division One	

DROP OR THREE OF CLARET

In March 2010, Wolves played three successive games against teams in claret and blue. After three successive defeats, Wolves beat Burnley 2-1 at Turf Moor before travelling to Villa Park and claiming a 2-2 draw just four days later. The treble was completed with a 3-1 win over West Ham at Molineux, which meant Wolves had taken seven points out of nine in the space of just eleven days. The earlier round of results saw a win over Burnley, another draw with Villa and a loss to West Ham at Upton Park meaning 11 points had been taken from a possible 18 against teams in those colours – more than a quarter of the 38 points taken in total all season.

WOLVES MANAGERS –
A COMPLETE HISTORY

Here are the men who have been in the Molineux hot seat since day one of the club's existence:

1885–1922 Jack Addenbroke

Games: 1,125
Won: 455
Drawn: 220
Lost: 450
Win ratio: 40.4 per cent

Jack Addenbroke enjoyed an almost 40-year association with Wolves. He joined as a goalkeeper in the 1880s and became secretary/manager, guiding the team to the 1889 FA Cup final where Preston won 3-0. He took Wolves back to the final in 1893 and this time returned to the Black Country with the trophy after a 1-0 win over Everton at Fallowfield in South Manchester. Addenbroke's penchant for the competition meant Wolves were finalists again three years later, losing 2-1 to Sheffield Wednesday at The Crystal Palace in front of almost 50,000 fans, but he made it to a fourth final in 1908, securing the FA Cup for the second time with a 3-1 win over Newcastle United – once again at The Crystal Palace – and this time watched by 74,967 fans. His fifth and final FA Cup final was in 1921, but Spurs triumphed 1-0 at Old Trafford. The first 18 seasons were in the top flight and his best finish was third on two occasions. After relegation in 1906, Addenbroke failed to win promotion but the club were relegated to the Third Division (North) for the first time the year after he left.

1922–24 George Jobey

Games: 91
Won: 36
Drawn: 26
Lost: 29
Win ratio: 39.6 per cent

After a successful playing career with several top clubs, George Jobey became Wolves' second manager in 1922 after Jack Addenbroke's 37-year reign finally came to an end. Jobey's first year in charge saw the club relegated to the third tier, but he then guided the club to the Division Three title – Wolves' first – at the first attempt. A tough disciplinarian, Jobey's reign was largely with an iron fist. However, his departure after just two years in charge was still something of a surprise as he elected to run a hotel instead, before returning in 1925 as Derby County boss.

1924–26 Albert Hoskins

Games: 78
Won: 34
Drawn: 13
Lost: 31
Win ratio: 43.6 per cent

Albert Hoskins worked his way to the top after beginning life as an office boy at Molineux. He learned his trade as an assistant to Jack Addenbrooke and took over as manager in May 1924 following George Jobey's departure. He guided Wolves to sixth and fourth place finishes before electing to sever his ties in the Black Country and instead take the job of secretary/manager at Gillingham in March 1926.

1926/27 Fred Scotchbrook

Games: 57
Won: 24
Drawn: 9
Lost: 24
Win ratio: 42.1 per cent

After being sacked as Stockport County boss, Fred Scotchbrook was the surprising choice by Wolves as the man to take over from Albert Hoskins. He helped steady the ship with six wins out of the final seven games, but his first full campaign began badly with no wins from the first ten games played. A strong run of results in the middle of the season meant relegation was comfortably avoided, but Scotchbrook became disillusioned with the interference of directors and left after making his views public after little more than a year at the helm.

1927–44 Maj. Frank Buckley

Games: 681
Won: 281

Drawn: 136
Lost: 264
Win ratio: 41.3 per cent

Born in Manchester, Maj. Frank Buckley served as a player with Aston Villa, Brighton, Manchester United, Manchester City, Birmingham, Derby County and Bradford City before the outbreak of war in 1914. After serving his country by joining up with the 17th Middlesex Regiment as an officer, he reached the rank of major in 1916 and commanded the 'Footballers Battalion', made up of soccer professionals. He became a popular figure and when he returned to football, he retained his name as Maj. Buckley, taking charge of Norwich, Blackpool and then Wolves. He was the perfect man to take the club to the next level and he guided Wolves to the Division Two title in 1932 after a steady year-on-year improvement. With a knack of spotting talented players, he built Wolves into a major force (pardon the pun), finishing runners up in Division One as well as reaching the 1939 FA Cup final where Portsmouth triumphed 4-1. Having brought in players such as Stan Cullis, Billy Wright, Jimmy Mullen and Dennis Westcott, it was cruel that the Second World War broke out just as Wolves were set for great things. Innovative and larger than life, Buckley stepped down as manager in 1944 when chairman Ben Mathews left his post.

1944–48 Ted Vizard

Games: 178
Won: 87
Drawn: 40
Lost: 51
Win ratio: 48.9 per cent

Ted Vizard spent the majority of his playing career with Bolton, making 512 appearances and scoring 70 goals. After spells in charge of Swindon Town and QPR, he won the post at Molineux after beating nearly 100 other applicants. However, the highlight of his rather unremarkable reign was finishing third in his first season after the cessation of the war. Though he managed another fifth-place finish the season after, he was replaced by assistant Stan Cullis who had served his apprenticeship by that point and was ready to take the helm.

1948–64 Stan Cullis

Games: 748
Won: 350
Drawn: 171
Lost: 227
Win ratio: 46.8 per cent

One of Wolves' greatest players would also become of the club's greatest managers, and few could have predicted how successful Stan Cullis would be as he embarked on his first managerial adventure at Molineux. The former Wolves and England skipper was probably promised the manager's job when he was persuaded to stay at Molineux following Hull City's approach in 1946. His appointment two years later proved an inspired one as Wolves entered a glorious period under his tutelage, winning League titles in the 1953/54, 1957/58 and 1958/59 seasons with perhaps the club's greatest team. Wolves also won the FA Cup in 1949 and 1960 as well as finishing runners-up in the League on two more occasions. The FA Charity Shield and the FA Youth Cup were also added to the list of successes before a gradual decline in the early 1960s cost him his job – much to the chagrin of the Wolverhampton public who adored him. After a short spell out of football, he returned to management with Birmingham City and enjoyed a few successful seasons before calling time on his career in 1970.

1964/65 Andy Beattie

Games: 44
Won: 19
Drawn: 7
Lost: 18
Win ratio: 43.2 per cent

Andy Beattie took control of Wolves partway through the 1964/65 campaign and left barely a year later. A former Scottish international, Beattie had a nomadic playing career that saw him enter management before the war with Barrow before moving on to Blackpool and then Huddersfield. He was twice Scotland's national team manager while also taking the helm at Carlisle, Nottingham Forest and Plymouth before taking over at Wolves. His methods soon raised questions, however, and his use of 28 players during his first season resulted in relegation from the top flight. Beattie quit after a 9-3 defeat to Southampton, partly due to his wife's poor health and partly perhaps because he already felt he'd done all he could for Wolves.

1965–68 Ronnie Allen

Games: 150
Won: 66
Drawn: 35
Lost: 49
Win ratio: 44.0 per cent

Ronnie Allen had an immediate effect on Wolves after taking over from Andy Beattie as he oversaw four successive 3-0 victories – one of the best starts by any Wolves boss. A West Brom legend, having scored 231 goals in 457 first team appearances for the Baggies, he knew he had to hit the ground running at Molineux. Allen signed Mike Bailey and Derek Dougan after narrowly missing out on promotion in his first campaign. He took Wolves back to the top flight the following season, lasting one more campaign before being shown the door after a poor run in the League.

1968–76 Bill McGarry

Games: 398
Won: 153
Drawn: 110
Lost: 135
Win ratio: 38.4 per cent

Bill McGarry had a steady, if unspectacular, playing career before becoming Bournemouth's first player-manager and then managed Watford and Ipswich Town before taking over as Wolves boss in November 1968. He proved a popular manager and his teams played solid, workmanlike football resulting in several notable successes including the Texaco Cup, a UEFA Cup final and a first League Cup triumph in 1974 after a win over Manchester City before he was sacked in 1976 following relegation from the top flight.

1976–78 Sammy Chung

Games: 108
Won: 41
Drawn: 27
Lost: 40
Win ratio: 38.0 per cent

Former Reading, Watford and Norwich player Sammy Chung had been player coach at Ipswich Town before moving to Molineux with Bill McGarry. After McGarry's dismissal, Chung was given the chance to branch out on his own and he guided Wolves to the Division Two title at the first time of asking. However, a season of consolidation was followed by a poor run of results that cost him his job in November 1978.

1978–82 John Barnwell

Games: 166
Won: 64
Drawn: 40
Lost: 62
Win ratio: 38.6 per cent

John Barnwell had enjoyed a fine playing career before moving into management at Hereford United. From there he moved to Peterborough United before succeeding Sammy Chung at Wolves. Barnwell steadied the ship as best he could, but Wolves were lucky to avoid the drop in his first season, though there was at least the distraction of a run to the semi-final of the FA Cup, where Barnwell was beaten by one of his former clubs, Arsenal. After surviving a horrific car crash, he returned to guide Wolves to sixth in the table in 1979/80 as well as winning the League Cup, having cleverly sold Steve Daley and brought in Aston Villa striker Andy Gray for the same record fee of £1.5 million. Barnwell again guided Wolves to the FA Cup semi-finals in 1981, but again it was a North London club, Spurs, who ended dreams of glory – incidentally, both Arsenal and Spurs went on to win the cup. A poor finish in the League and dreadful run the season after saw Barnwell controversially sacked in January 1982; refusing to pen a new deal brought the end to his colourful reign at Molineux.

1982 Ian Greaves

Games: 20
Won: 5
Drawn: 6
Lost: 9
Win ratio: 25.0 per cent

There is little positive to say of Ian Greaves' brief reign as manager of Wolves. He enjoyed a successful spell at Bolton before eventually being sacked. With just 5 wins from 20, it seemed inevitable he would suffer the same fate at Molineux after failing to keep the club in the top flight – and did – following Derek Dougan's takeover.

1982–84 Graham Hawkins

Games: 90
Won: 26
Drawn: 28
Lost: 36
Win ratio: 28.9 per cent

Though Graham Hawkins guided Wolves straight back up to Division One at his first attempt, he would also be the manager who immediately took the club back down at the start of a yo-yo period that would spark an incredible drop through the divisions. A former Wolves player, he never established himself in the first-team and after four years, he moved to Preston where he fared better and eventually joined Blackburn Rovers. After a spell with Port Vale, he became assistant manager at Shrewsbury Town and was something of a surprise choice when new chief executive Derek Dougan employed him in 1982. After finishing runners-up to QPR and winning promotion in 1983, he then found the top flight an entirely different beast and Wolves' nosedive towards relegation saw him lose his job in April 1984 with caretaker Jim Barron unable to halt the slide.

1984–85 Tommy Docherty

Games: 48
Won: 9

Drawn: 12
Lost: 27
Win ratio: 18.8 per cent

One of football's most colourful characters, Tommy Docherty arguably had his best years long before he took over at ailing Wolves. 'The Doc' enjoyed his best years with Manchester United, though he managed Chelsea, Rotherham, QPR, Aston Villa and Scotland before taking over at Old Trafford. After winning the FA Cup with the Reds in 1977 and losing the final again a couple of years later, he moved on to Derby, QPR (again) and Preston after a brief spell Down Under. Wolves believed he had the charisma to halt the slide down the leagues, but Wolves' second straight relegation after finishing rock bottom of Division Two and entering the third tier of English football for only the second time meant The Doc was duly shown the door.

1985/86 Sammy Chapman

Games: 33
Won: 8
Drawn: 9
Lost: 16
Win ratio: 24.2 per cent

Sammy Chapman held the fort until Bill McGarry returned to Molineux, which means, chronologically, he came before McGarry's second coming. He oversaw a handful of games before making way for the legendary former boss. He would then be offered the post after just 12 games of McGarry's reign, but, despite bookending the 1985/86 campaign, Chapman was unable to prevent a record third consecutive relegation. Wolves' first ever stint in Division Four saw the sixth managerial casualty in less than five years.

1985 Bill McGarry

Games: 12
Won: 2
Drawn: 3
Lost: 7
Win ratio: 16.7 per cent

Bill McGarry lasted just 61 days on his second spell at the club, but couldn't save the club, which he realised fairly quickly, stepping aside to let Chapman have a go.

1986–94 Graham Turner

Games: 412
Won: 179
Drawn: 109
Lost: 124
Win ratio: 43.4 per cent

Brian Little took caretaker control of Wolves until Graham Turner took the helm. Little presided over three wins in 36 days as Wolves attampted to climb back up the League ladder. Turner had played all his football along the Welsh border with Wrexham, Chester and Shrewsbury before becoming player/boss of the latter. He guided the Shrews to the Division Three title and also reached the sixth round of the FA Cup before continuing his meteoric rise by accepting the post of Aston Villa manager. Turner was sacked, but found solace a few miles away at Wolves where he was handed the challenge of waking a slumbering giant. He signed Steve Bull and guided Wolves to the play-offs, but his second campaign saw the Division Four title secured as well as the Sherpa Van Troph. The season after saw Wolves promoted back to Division Two, meaning the club had been in a different division for eight of the previous nine years! Turner managed three mid-table finishes before being replaced in March 1994, safe in the knowledge he'd played a major role in winning the club some much-needed pride back.

1994/95 Graham Taylor

Games: 91
Won: 36
Drawn: 29
Lost: 28
Win ratio: 39.6 per cent

With his record at Watford still fresh in the mind of football folk, Graham Taylor seemed the ideal man to continue where Turner had left off. Taylor had taken Watford from Division Four to the summit of Division One during a meteoric decade at Vicarage Road. Taylor then moved to Aston Villa where he won promotion back to the top flight, narrowly avoided immediate relegation and then finished runners-up to Liverpool in successive seasons. All of which brought him to the attention of England, which turned out to be something of a disaster for the popular club manager. He arrived at Molineux in April 1994 and very nearly took the club up via the play-offs, losing to Bolton in the semi-final over two legs. His stay in the Black Country was to be brief, however, and just eight months later he was sacked after a poor run.

1995–98 Mark McGhee

Games: 159
Won: 65
Drawn: 39
Lost: 55
Win ratio: 40.9 per cent

After staving off relegation in his first five months in charge, Mark McGhee began to rebuild the team with one or two experienced campaigners. However, with poor luck on the pitch and worse off it, with several key players ruled out with long-term injuries, the fifth-place finish in the Championship would surely have been higher, but it was Crystal Palace who ended the promotion dream, winning 4-3 over two legs. After a decent start to the 1997/98 campaign, injuries again took their toll and McGhee's contract was terminated after an eventful stay in the Black Country.

1998–2000 Colin Lee

Games: 111
Won: 44
Drawn: 33
Lost: 34
Win ratio: 39.6 per cent

Colin Lee initially took on the post in a caretaker capacity, but he was soon offered the hot seat on a permanent basis. He began his reign with a 6-1 win at Bristol City plus two more wins and a draw –

enough to convince the board to give him the job. Wolves just missed out on promotion at the end of his first (half) season in charge. Sadly, such appointments are always skating on thin ice and the first real hiccup of his time in charge was met with the sack.

2001–04 Dave Jones

Games: 187
Won: 75
Drawn: 53
Lost: 60
Win ratio: 40.1 per cent

After cutting his teeth with a succession of non-League northern clubs, Dave Jones became Stockport County boss after working his way up through the backroom staff. He guided County to the Championship and the semi-final of the Coca-Cola Cup before being snapped up by Southampton where a court case interrupted his career indefinitely. Cleared of all charges, Jones returned to management with Wolves after almost a year out of the game. After arriving in January 2001, he guided the club to a mid-table finish. He guided the club to the play-offs a year later, losing to Norwich City in the semi-finals. However, 12 months later, Jones led Wolves to promotion to the Premier League for the first time since its inception, following a 3-0 win over Sheffield United at Cardiff's Millennium Stadium. The return to the Promised Land lasted just one season and a poor start to the 2004/05 season saw him sacked in November.

2004–06 Glenn Hoddle

Games: 76
Won: 27
Drawn: 34
Lost: 15
Win ratio: 35.5 per cent

Glenn Hoddle began his management career by taking third-tier Swindon Town to the Premier League against all the odds and was soon headhunted by Chelsea. After three moderately successful years at Stamford Bridge, he was offered the England job, guiding the nation to the 1998 World Cup finals, but England were knocked out on penalties by Argentina. His personal beliefs and odd statements during an interview with *The Times* saw him sacked as England boss in February 1999, later taking on the role as Southampton boss where, ironically, Dave Jones had just left, and remained on the south coast until he was offered the Spurs job in March 2001. There was to be no fairytale at The Lane and he left after two average campaigns, taking over as Wolves manager after the sacking of Jones. Wolves went on a superb run, losing just once in 25 games, but too many draws – 15 – meant the late surge for the play-offs was in vain, and his second season again saw the club fall just short of the play-offs. Hoddle resigned six weeks after the season ended, stating, 'I feel my expectations and the club's have drifted too far apart and this decision has been made early for the benefit of the club.' And that was that.

2006–12 Mick McCarthy

Games: 270
Won: 104
Drawn: 66
Lost: 100
Win ratio: 38.5 per cent

Mick McCarthy arrived promising promotion within three seasons of him taking over. He cleverly weaved some astute bargain buys with promising youth-team graduates and almost achieved a return to the Premier League at the first attempt, losing out to West Brom in the semi-finals of the play-offs. The following campaign saw Wolves edged out of the play-offs by goal difference, meaning he had to succeed at the third attempt to fulfil his prophecy. McCarthy was true to his word, and a classy Wolves secured promotion in mid-April, clinching the Championship title the following week having topped the table for all but four weeks of the campaign. McCarthy then steered Wolves to Premier League safety, something he hadn't managed in two previous attempts with Sunderland and a fifteenth-place finish represented a very good season. A dramatic end to McCarthy's fifth season at the helm saw safety achieved again, but only after results elsewhere condemned others to the drop, meaning the Yorkshireman had become the first Wolves boss in 30 years to secure successive top-flight campaigns. There was surprise when McCarthy was sacked during his sixth season at Molineux with poor form costing him his job. He remains one of the most popular Wolves managers of the modern era.

2012 Terry Connor

Games: 13
Won: 0
Drawn: 4
Lost: 9
Win ratio: 0.0 per cent

Terry Connor was the surprise choice to take over from Mick McCarthy. The assistant boss had no experience of management and to be thrown into the middle of a relegation battle proved too much for the likeable Connor, who failed to win any of his 13 games in charge as Wolves were relegated with a 2-0 defeat at Molineux by Manchester City.

2012/13 Stale Solbakken

Games: 30
Won: 10
Drawn: 5
Lost: 15
Win ratio: 33.3 per cent

Stale Solbakken lasted barely six months as Wolves manager, but what did we really know about the former Norwegian international? Stale played a handful of games for Wimbledon under the tutelage of Joe Kinnear. His playing career began in his native land, ending up with Lillestrom in the top League where he won a midfielder of the year award in 1995. A move to Premier League Wimbledon followed, but after six games he fell out with Kinnear and was banned from the club. A move back to Scandinavia followed when he joined Aalborg in Denmark, where again a player of the season award was won as he lead the team to the title in 1999. A move to the capital club FC Copenhagen in 2000 was meant to lead to even bigger things, working under future England manager Roy Hodgson. After only

14 games, Stale suffered a heart-attack in training, aged only 33. His heart had stopped and he was revived in the ambulance. This lead to the need for a pacemaker to be fitted and the end of his playing career, having also won 58 caps for Norway. Sadly, with just 10 wins from 30 games, it didn't work out at Molineux and Stale was shown the door, returning to manage FC Copenhagen in 2013. His win ration was exactly one in three having managed Wolves in 30 games, 10 of which ended in victory, five were draws and 15 ended in defeat.

2013 Dean Saunders

Games: 20
Won: 5
Drawn: 5
Lost: 10
Win ratio: 25.0 per cent

Dean Saunders' reign was just long enough for Wolves to complete yet another back-to-back relegation. The Welshman inherited a team on a downward spiral and when he couldn't stop it, the board opted for a change in direction and sacked him.

2013–present Kenny Jackett

Games: 81
Won: 43
Drawn: 23
Lost: 15
Win ratio: 53.1 per cent

When Kenny Jackett left Millwall after six years, Wolves believed they had the prefect man to guide the club back to the top flight. The quietly spoken boss wasted no time in shaping a team in his image and Wolves were crowned with the League One title at the first attempt. At the time of writing (October 2014), Wolves were challenging in the play-off positions of the Championship. Looks like this Jackett is the perfect fit!

(Record correct as of 30 January 2015)

THE FIRST EVER GAME

The first official match at Molineux was Wolves *v.* Aston Villa on 2 September 1889. The referee was Charles Crump, with almost 4,000 fans in attendance. At precisely 5.30 p.m. the game began and Wolves were officially off and running. David Wykes scored the only goal of the game to write his name in history (as this book proves) with Villa 'keeper Jack Warner to blame as he allowed the ball to squeeze through his fingers and into the net. Wolves played in red-and-white stripes!

The Wolves team was as follows: W. Rose, R. Baugh, C. Mason, A. Fletcher, H. Allen, T. Knight, A. Worrall, W. Perry, D. Wykes, H. Wood, C. Booth.

Major rule differences at the time, some bizarre, included the following:

1. The 'keeper could go anywhere on the pitch and handle the ball.

2. There were no penalties.

3. There were two umpires instead of a referee, and they had flags not whistles.

4. There were no goal nets and no crossbar, only a rope.

5. When the ball crossed the touchline for a throw-in, the first player to reach the ball was entitled to take the throw, and could throw it one-handed.

6. The goalkeeper could be barged by other players, whether or not he was in possession of the ball.

LEGEND: ANDY GRAY

Full Name: Andrew Mullen Gray
Born: 30 November 1955 in Glasgow

Andy scored over 200 goals in 620 matches during a brilliant career beginning in 1970 with Clydebank Strollers. He turned professional with Dundee United in May 1973 and played 75 games for them. In 1974, he collected a Scottish Cup runner-up medal. In 1975, he transferred from Tannadice Park to Villa Park for £110,000 and scored 69 goals in 141 matches during his spell with Aston Villa.

He signed for Wolves on 8 September 1979 for £1,469,000 and became the most expensive footballer in Britain just days after

Wolves midfielder Steve Daley had joined Manchester City for a few pounds less. Gray's debut for Wolves was a 3-2 victory over Everton at Goodison Park on 15 September 1979, in which he scored his first of 45 goals for Wolves with his most memorable effort the winning goal against Nottingham Forest at Wembley in the 1980 League Cup final – ensuring he attained the status of a club great, even if his time in the Black Country was destined to be all too brief.

Injuries kept Gray out of a third of the next season's games. He then left Molineux in November 1983, going to Everton for a bargain £250,000. He scored 14 goals in 49 League appearances and collected winners medals in three different competitions; First Division, FA Cup and European Cup Winners Cup. In July 1985, he returned to Aston Villa for £150,000, before moving on to Notts County on loan and also spent 12 months at West Brom on loan.

He finished his top-flight career with boyhood idols Rangers, helping them to the Scottish Premier League title and Skol Cup triumphs. Rangers released him at the end of the 1988/89 season and he joined non-League Cheltenham Town. He also began a new career as a sports presenter, which he still does to this day.

LET THERE BE LIGHT

In the summer of 1953, the first set of floodlights was lifted into position at Molineux. They were officially switched on later that year when a South Africa national team came over to play a friendly on 30 September. Wolves then embarked on a series of floodlit friendly matches, beating Racing Club of Buenos Aires 3-1, Dynamo Moscow 2-1 and Spartak Moscow 4-0. However, the game perhaps best remembered was the clash against top Hungarian side Honved. Hungary, led by the legendary Ferenc Puskas, had beaten England 6-3 at Wembley in November 1953 and the following summer emphasised their superiority by winning 7-1 in Budapest. With English football at a low, the match between Wolves and Honved took on a new meaning and at half-time the Hungarians led 2-0. Wolves, however, were far from finished and fought back to win 3-2 to the delight of the packed home crowd and, in winning, restored pride to English football, which had taken something of a battering.

CLUB BADGE

Wolves have one of the most recognizable and striking club badges not only in British football, but the world – and that's no exaggeration. Wolves' badge does exactly what it says on the tin – namely, a wolf.

Going back in history, pre-war shirts were very plain, with no club badges, sponsor's logo or manufacturer's logo. It wasn't until the 1950s that Wolves began using the town's coat of arms – but it was only on special occasions such as Cup Finals, like the 1960 FA Cup final, when the Wolverhampton coat of arms was used.

In the late 1960s, Wolves started using a single leaping wolf with the two W's above on their shirts for every match; it was positioned on the left-hand breast side. That was followed by the three leaping wolves in the middle of the shirt – one of the club's most popular of all time. In 1980, the club started using the single wolf's head, and they had various designs of this. Then in the 1994/95 season they swapped back to using the town's coat of arms along with the wolf's head but only for that season, swapping back to the familiar single wolf's head. It's likely there will be tweaks in years to come, but you can't improve on perfection!

LEGEND: JIMMY MURRAY

1955–63
Appearances: 273
Goals: 199
Position: Striker
Born: Dover

Jimmy Murray was signed up by Wolves as a youngster and turned professional in November 1953. He spent a few seasons plying his trade in the reserves before he finally made his League debut on 12 November 1955 in a 2–0 win over Charlton Athletic.

He quickly established himself within the team that season, scoring 11 goals and remained a prolific scorer for the club over the following seasons. In 1957/58, Murray was the leading goalscorer as the club captured the League title. Murray also won an FA Cup winners' medal in 1960 after playing in the 3–0 final win over Blackburn Rovers.

Wolves benefited greatly from the scoring prowess of Murray as he bagged 199 goals in 273 League games for the Molineux side.

No wonder then, that new Manchester City manager George Poyser should target the Dover-born forward as the man to steer his club back out of Division Two at the first attempt. Having already signed the prolific Derek Kevan from Chelsea, the pair went on to forge a prolific partnership for City.

THE DEMISE OF STEVE DALEY

Steve Daley joined Manchester City from Wolverhampton Wanderers for £1,437,500 in 1979 to become the most expensive British signing ever. Malcolm Allison saw Daley as the perfect player to build his young side around, but things went horribly wrong. It was hardly his fault, but Daley never looked anywhere near like a player worth the fee City had paid. The huge sum seemed to weigh heavily on his shoulders and he soon became the target of discontent from fans who saw him as a waste of precious funds. He had looked an industrious midfielder with ability at Molineux, but the move to Maine Road sent his career spiraling into reverse. After 15 months of disappointment for all concerned, he signed for US club Seattle Sounders for a fraction of the fee paid for his services. For Wolves fans, it was a mystery why a player on the verge of international honours should lose his way so badly – but his transfer funded the record purchase of Andy Gray shortly after, so all was not lost.

POTTERS BOTHER

Due to the gradual fall from grace of their main geographical rivals Port Vale, Stoke City fans have deemed it necessary to place more emphasis on the games against Wolves as the two clubs play each other more frequently in the League. There is a history of hooligan activity surrounding this game, which adds to the often intense atmosphere when the two teams meet. It is a derby, but not like most same-town derbies. The first 15 meetings between the clubs saw Wolves win ten and draw three, losing just twice. Of the 149 meetings to date, Wolves have won 64, drawn 35 and lost 50 meaning that almost two thirds of the meetings have ended with a positive result for the Gold and Blacks.

LET THERE BE (MORE) LIGHT

Bristol City have always found Wolves to be illuminating opposition. Quite literally in fact. In 1952, inventor and Bristol club chairman Harry Dolman spent the summer months working in his factory at Pennywell Road, Euston, designing the first set of floodlights for Ashton Gate. After being commissioned for £3,500, Dolman's floodlights were no more than tall metal poles with clusters of lights fixed to the top, but on 27 January 1953 the makeshift floodlights were turned on for the first time at a City home game – a friendly against Wolverhampton Wanderers – a groundbreaking event in the history of British football. Though Wolves won 4-1, a bumper crowd of 24,008 had turned out for the novelty of a match played at night. In 1965, after the Robins won promotion to Division Two after finishing runners-up in Division Three, their new 'proper' floodlights were switched on for the first time during a friendly against – you guessed it – Wolves. So the first two floodlit games, new and old and 12 years apart, were against the Gold and Blacks – the same club the Robins played during Ashton Gate's first floodlit game 12 years earlier! It seems, whenever Bristol City acquire new lights, the Wolves are literally at the door!

COLLAPSE IF YOU LOVE THE WOLVES

Normally we wouldn't bother with a testimonial for a former West Brom player, but on this occasion, we'll make an exception. Steve Bull caused plenty of smiles when he took part in Bob Taylor's testimonial in 2003. The Baggies' legend invited Bull to play in the game between Albion and a team of ex-Albion players at The Hawthorns.

More than 16,000 turned out for the game, which the current Albion side won 7-2, but Bully played the first half for his former employers and, when a chant of 'Stand up if you love the Wolves' echoed around the ground, Bully collapsed to the ground in protest, much to the amusement of all concerned. Wolves till he dies!

The teams that day were as follows:

ALBION: Hoult (Crane HT [Taylor 80]); Sigurdsson (Collins HT), Wallwork (Dyer HT), J. Chambers; Lyttle, McInnes, Koumas (Roberts 75), Johnson (Mkandawire HT), Clement (Rev Hipkiss 84); Roberts (Dobie HT), Taylor (Hughes 27 [Brown HT]).

BRYAN ROBSON'S ALLSTARS: Flowers (Jensen HT); Hamilton (Hackett 71), Palmer, Adams, Trewick (Fereday 7); G. Robson, B. Robson (Regis 78), Sneekes, Flynn (Lilwall 71); Bull (Hughes HT), Goodman (O'Kelly 78).
Attendance: 16,017

STAIRWAY TO MOLINEUX

Led Zeppelin rock god Robert Plant – maybe Wolves' most famous fan – can't hide his love for the Gold and Black boys as he proves with these quotes:

> Bully jumped me once, against Bolton at the Reebok, and shouted 'Here's Planty, who's this then?' He brought the place together with his charisma, with the way he'd leave two defenders behind him knocking heads with each other, and the way he would run back and dispossess an opponent while our midfield looked on in sleepy awe.

> The dynamics of life. Looking back is very convenient because you can't actually really quantify the changes and the twists and turns.
> I had a really bad car wreck. I was in a wheelchair for yonks and little did I know that as I learned to walk again at the Molineux – Wolverhampton Wanderers helped me in physiotherapy.
> I was on sticks after seven months. I went back there and I started training with the team – with John Richards and Kenny Hibbitt and all those people and had a wonderful time. And maybe once I got some measure of motion and stuff back, was back on my feet – literally.

LEGEND: GEOFF PALMER

1973–84 and 1985–87
Appearances: 489 and 7
Goals: 15

Geoff Palmer fully deserves to be called a Wolverhampton Wanderers legend, with 17 years of service under his belt and appearing in just four games short of 500.

Palmer was a dyed-in-the-wool Wolves fan from a young boy, and it was fitting that he ended up playing for the club he loved for the majority of his career.

He had an unusual debut in that it was in the ill-fated FA Cup third and fourth place play-off – yes, they really did trial that nonsense of an idea for a couple of years – against Arsenal in August 1973.

A Cannock lad, he'd joined as an apprentice in 1970 and after breaking into the senior team, he soon became a permanent fixture at right-back. He was part of the Wolves side that won the 1974 League Cup against Manchester City and was part of two Wolves squads that won promotion from Division Two.

After a decade of sterling service, Palmer was awarded a testimonial in 1983 and joined Burnley in December 1984 for £5,000.

Palmer would make just 34 appearances for the Clarets before returning to Molineux in December 1985, where he made a further 22 starts for the Gold and Blacks.

Palmer retired in 1987 and spent more than 20 years in the West Midlands police force where he continued to play for a representative side in the Midland Combination for a number of years. After 23 years, Palmer retired from the police but still leaves close to his beloved Wolves where he is a regular attender.

MAKE MINE A TREBLE

Harry Wood became the first Wolves player to score a Football League hat-trick in November 1888 when he bagged a treble during a 4-1 win over Derby County. Wood played for Wolves between 1885 and 1898 and the three goals were just a fraction of the 126 he scored in total during 289 appearances.

OLDEST AND YOUNGEST

The current record holders for the oldest and youngest players to represent Wolves are as follows: Lawrie Madden was 37 years old 222 days when he last played for Wolves in May 1993, whereas the youngest was Jimmy Mullen who was just 16 years 41 days when he made his debut against Leeds United in February 1939 during a 4-1 win. However, the unofficial record holder for being the youngest player goes to Cameron Buchanan, who had just turned 14 two months earlier when he played for Wolves on Boxing Day 1942 against West Brom – unfortunately, because it was during the Second World War, the record doesn't count. Shame, because while Mullen and Madden's records will probably be beaten at some point, it's hard to imagine anyone younger than Buchanan wearing gold and black.

CAN YOU HEAR US ON THE BOX?

For those lucky enough to own a TV, 14 November 1964 was a day to remember if you were a Wolves fan, as a whole new world opened up as *Match of the Day* screened the 3-1 Molineux win over Spurs – the first time Wolves had appeared on national TV for a highlights show. Goals from Crawford, Le Fern and Wharton did the trick in front of almost 29,000 fans.

LEGEND: ANDY MUTCH

1986–93
Appearances: 288
Goals: 106
Position: Striker
Born: Liverpool

Andy Mutch spent most of his Wolves career in the sizeable shadow of Steve Bull – not to say that he wasn't appreciated by the Wolves fans, because he was – it was just that Bull's extraordinary scoring prowess stole all the headlines. The truth was, Bull was at his most prolific when Mutch was his striker partner and the pair can quite rightly claim to have been the club's greatest ever strike duo. Mutch's individual record is right up there with some of the Wolves greats, and there was a time when it seemed only Mutch or Bull scored for Wolves.

A former trainee with both Liverpool and Everton, Mutch eventually found a home in Southport FC, staying with the non-League outfit from 1984 to 1986. Then, Wolves gave him the break he had been looking for when they signed the 20-year-old striker for the final few months of the 1987/87 campaign. Despite scoring seven goals in 15 games, he couldn't prevent Wolves slipping into the bottom division.

His first full season in black and gold, however, proved an unqualified success as Steve Bull arrived at the club eight months after Mutch and Bull helped Wolves into the 1986/87 play-offs, narrowly missing out on promotion. Mutch and Bull were unstoppable the following campaign, as Wolves steamrollered their way to the title thanks in no small part to the 53 League goals scored by the dynamic duo, with Mutch on the scoresheet in the 2-0 Sherpa Van Trophy win over Burnley in May 1988.

Wolves made it back-to-back titles in 1988/89 as the club won Division Three with Mutch and Bull banging in 58 goals between them, and an incredible 83 in all competitions – an amazing record. The only regret of Mutch's time at Molineux was that he never managed to represent the club in the top flight having spent the next five years attempting to win a third promotion. During his time in the Black Country he won three England B caps and also won England Under-21 honours before he finally got his wish of playing in the Premier League following a £250,000 move to Swindon Town.

Mutch had scored 106 goals in 288 appearances for Wolves, and he deserves his place among the club greats for helping restore the Black and Golds to the periphery of the top division once again.

FA CUP THIRD/FOURTH PLACE PLAY-OFF

Between 1970 and 1974, the FA, in its infinite wisdom, came up with the idea that a third and fourth place play-off would be a good idea for the losing FA Cup semi-finalists. It's hard to think of a more pointless game, but it's an indication of the high esteem the competition was held in during that period.

The first game took place in 1970 as Manchester United beat Watford 2-0 at Highbury, but the crowd of just 15,000 should have been an indicator that all was not well. Nonetheless, the FA persisted. However, when just 5,031 turned out to see Stoke beat Everton at Selhurst Park, it should have sounded the death knell for a game none but the most diehard of supporters were interested in.

The game was switched to one of the competing teams the season after, and as Birmingham beat Stoke on penalties at St Andrews in August 1972, the fact that 26,000-plus had attended perhaps saved the game for a little longer and in 1973, enter Wolves' only match in the experimental fixture. It turned out well, with Bill McGarry's side winning 3-1 against Arsenal at Higbury in front of just over 21,000. Two goals from Derek Dougan and another from Jim McCalliog meant Wolves finished third in the competition for the only time.

Burnley and Leicester contested the last third/fourth place game the season after, but when less than 7,000 watched the Clarets triumph 1-0 at Filbert Street, it was finally decided there was no appetite for the game.

THREE IS THE MAGIC NUMBER

Wolves and Stoke contested the shortest game on record in 1894 when the two teams kicked off in wintry conditions. Things deteriorated quickly and a fierce blizzard made it impossible to continue the game, so the official called a halt with just 3 minutes played and the score, not surprisingly, was still 0-0. The 400 hardy souls who had turned out left the ground shivering and probably relieved.

SONGS

Here are some terrace favourites, past and present that Wolves fans have sung for one reason or another. Some are long gone, some are quite recent and some have been sung for many decades.

'Greatest Team in the Land'

Oh Wolves are the greatest team of the land,
We wear the gold and black scarf in our hands,
We're in the lead, we're in the lead, we're in the lead!!
We're in the lead, we're in the lead, we're in the lead!!
Oh Wolves are the best team who ever played
And We will never never never never fade
We're in the lead, we're in the lead, we're in the lead!!
We're in the lead, we're in the lead, we're in the lead!!
The Wanderers are in the lead la, la, la, laaaaaaaa!

'Those Were the Days'

Once upon a time, there was a tavern,
Where we used to raise a glass or two, or three or four!
Where we used to while away the hours,
Thinking of the things we used to do.
Those were the days my friend, we thought they'd never end,
We'd sing and dance forever and a day.
We'd live the live we choose,
We'd fight and never lose,
For we're The Wolves, oh yes we are The Wolves!
La la la la la. La la la la
La la la laaa la, la la la la …

'Stevie Bull's a Tatter'

Stevie Bull's a tatter
He wears an England cap
He plays for Wolverhampton
And he's a lovely chap

He scores with his left foot
He scores with his right
And when we play the Albion
He'll score all f***ing night
WOOOOOHHH
Stevie Bull's a tatter … (etc.)

'I Was Born (Under a Wand'rers Scarf)'

I was born under a Wand'rers scarf
I was born under a Wand'rers scarf
Do you know where hell is? Hell is at West Brom
Heaven is at Molineux and that's where we come from
I was born under a Wand'rers scarf…

'Oh When The Wolves'

Oh when the Wolves (oh when the Wolves)
Go marching in (go marching in)
Oh when the Wolves go marching in;
I want to be in that number,
When the Wolves go marching in…

'Glory, Glory Wolverhampton'

Glory Glory Wolverhampton
Glory Glory Wolverhampton
Glory Glory Wolverhampton
And Wolves go marching ON ON ON

'We Love You Wanderers (We Do)'

We love you Wanderers, we do
We love you Wanderers, we do
We love you Wanderers, we do
Oh, Wanderers we love you…
Fight, fight wherever you may be
Fight, fight wherever you may be
We are the boys of the Black Country
And we'll beat you all, wherever you may be
We are the boys of the Black Country

'Follow The Wanderers'

We will follow the Wanderers over land and sea,
We will follow the Wanderers, on to victory
All together now, repeat.

'Keep the Gold Flag Flying High'

We'll Never Die,
We'll Never Die,
We'll Never Die,
We'll Never Die,
Wanderers Will Never Die,
We'll Keep The Gold Flag Flying High…

'The Boys of the Black Country'

Fight, fight,
Where ever you may be,
We are the boys of the black country,
And we'll beat you all wherever you may be,
We are the boys of the Black Country …

'White Pelé'

I saw my mate the other day,
He said to me he saw the white Pelé,
So I asked who he is,

He goes by the name of Matt Jarvis,
Matt Jarvis, Matt Jarvis,
He goes by the name of Matt Jarvis,
Matt Jarvis, Matt Jarvis,
He goes by the name of Matt Jarvis…

WOLVES AT THE DOOR

Black Country cousins Albion and Wolves played both league derbies at The Hawthorns in 1919 following crowd disturbances at Molineux the season before. The Football League granted Wolves permission to switch to Albion's home ground while the problems on their own patch were investigated. In the meantime, Wolves lost 4-2 to Barnsley and drew 2-2 against Stockport County during their temporary two-game tenure.

SIR JACK HAYWARD 1923–2015

When Sir Jack Hayward died in January 2015, there was an outpouring of gratitude towards the former owner/chairman/life president.

It was Sir Jack who financed the complete rebuilding of Molineux and whose legacy goes far beyond the superb Premier League standard stadium Wolves are proud to call their home.

Born in the Dunstall area of Wolverhampton on 14 June 1923, Sir Jack followed Wolves from an early age and was a regular attender at Molineux before attending public school and then serving in the RAF during the Second World War.

He oversaw his father's business interests in several territories after the war and after marrying in 1948, he and his wife had two sons and a daughter. As his business empire grew, Sir Jack's generosity became the stuff of legend, purchasing land for the National Trust, restoring a treasured ship and making sizeable donations to worthy causes were just some of the philanthropic gestures he made.

He was awarded the OBE in 1968 and became Sir Jack in 1986. In May 1990, he finally bought the club he adored so much and during 17 years of ownership Sir Jack spent in the region of £70 million to redevelop the club and stadium. A decrepit, ageing Molineux slowly became the fine all-seater stadium it is today.

His dream of guiding Wolves to the Premier League came true in 2003, and in 2007 he sold the club for just £10 to Steve Morgan

– in return for a £30 million investment in the club. Though his day-to-day activity was over, he remained a diehard Wolves fan exiled in the Grand Bahamas, though attending when he could and was bestowed the honour of Life President by the club.

A road near Molineux was named Jack Hayward Way in his honour to celebrate his 80th birthday and whenever there has been a promotion or civic reception, Sir Jack was there to celebrate with all the other Wolves fans.

He passed away at the grand old age of 91, and is almost unique in his popularity among Wolves fans who greatly appreciated the benevolence and selflessness of their former owner. Sir Jack was a one-off and every bit a Wolves legend who will be sadly missed.

THE TWELFTH MAN

Fred Goodwin wrote a little piece of history when he replaced Ernie Hunt for Wolves against Middlesbrough on 16 October 1965. It was the first time a substitute had been used by Wolves and to mark the occasion, Wolves won the game 3-0.

TWO IN 60 SECONDS

As impossible as it may sound, the game between Wolves and Huddersfield Town in February 1933 yielded two goals – in the opening minute! Alf Young put the ball past his own 'keeper with just a few seconds gone, but, remarkably, the Terriers scored almost straight from the restart with a minute still not even played! It was an incredible start to the game, and to think even if you arrived at the ground at 3.01 p.m., you'd have still missed two goals! Still, there were plenty more to follow as Wolves edged a ten-goal thriller by winning 6-4 in front of 20,070 Molineux fans.

THE PERFECT TEN

Wolves recorded their biggest League win ever during the 1937/38 campaign when Leicester City were well and truly put to the sword at Molineux. There was no hint of what was to come before the game as two out-of-sorts sides went into the match looking to improve recent poor runs. Wolves had won once in seven outings while the Foxes, battling to avoid relegation, had one win in six. The visitors held out for

13 minutes before Dennis Westcott put Wolves ahead and Dicky Dorsett added three more before the break to give the hosts a comfortable 4-0 lead. Bryn Jones and Westcott made it 6-0 with 52 minutes on the clock and Teddy Maguire made it seven goals just past the hour. Sidlow scored an own goal to give Leicester some consolation, but Wolves were far from finished and Dorsett made it 8-1 on 83 minutes. Two minutes after that, Westcott made it 9-1. There was only 60 seconds remaining when Westcott scored his fourth to make it 10-1, much to the delight of the 22,540-strong home crowd. The teams met just three days later and the Foxes restored some pride with a 1-1 draw at Filbert Street.

NONE SHALL PASS

Wolves posted a new consecutive clean sheet record during the early weeks of the 1982/83 season. After opening the campaign with a 2-1 win over Blackburn Rovers, Wolves travelled to Chelsea and secured a 0-0 draw before taking another 0-0 draw at Leeds United – two solid defensive displays inside five days. Wolves then thrashed Charlton 5-0 at Molineux and followed that 2-0 win over Barnsley. On a roll, Graham Hawkins' side then secured an impressive 1-0 at Bolton Wanderers and backed up the superb form on the road with a 2-0 home win over Rotherham United. The long trip to Carlisle resulted in another 2-0 victory and the eighth League shutout in a row was achieved with a 0-0 draw at Sheffield Wednesday. Leicester City ended the proud run with a 3-0 win at Molineux and Cambridge United ended the sequence of five clean sheets on the road as the U's won 2-1 at the Abbey Stadium. 'Keeper John Burridge ended the campaign with 21 shutouts in all competitions – not a bad record.

CHAMPIONS OF THE WORLD!

You know how it works – you support a team who beat another team who in turn beat another team, who then beat a side regarded as one of the greatest ever. It's like Port Vale beating Stoke in a friendly, Stoke beating Chelsea who had just beaten Real Madrid so, technically, Port Vale must be a better team than Real Madrid. OK, it doesn't quite work like that, but you get the picture.

In 1954, Wolves fans had just cause to say their side was one of the best in the world, based on a friendly that had Molineux rocking and the nation's football writers purring. Heady days indeed! English football was still rocking from Hungary's 6-3 win at Wembley Stadium a year earlier and six months after an embarrassing 7-1 annihilation in Hungary that had left the nation stunned at the manner of the thrashings.

With Budapest's Honvéd back in England to bewitch the public once again, Wolves were delighted the Hungarians accepted the invitation to play at Molineux for a pre-Christmas friendly. With the BBC covering the game live and 55,000 packed into the stadium, the scene was set for a magical night under the floodlights.

Wolves went into the game as defending Division One champions and were again top of the pile by a point going into this game, which was in effect a precursor to the European Cup with two national champions facing each other in a game that was anything but a friendly. There was national pride at stake and everybody in England was willing Wolves to bring the magnificent Magyars down a peg or two.

The visitors included many Hungarian internationals, but it was the great Ferenc Puskás who was the player everyone wanted to see in the flesh. Having seen off Racing Club, First Vienna, Celtic, Maccabi Tel Aviv and Spartak Moscow, the Wolves fans had developed quite a taste for international friendlies, but this was one was extra special and it became obvious in the opening exchanges that Honvéd were a class apart. Their fluid and interchangeable formation bamboozled the Gold and Blacks in the early stages and with just 14 minutes gone the home fans feared the worst as Honvéd went 2-0 up.

The hosts reached the break having prevented further damage,but manager Stan Cullis had a theory that if the pitch surface became less slick and suited to Honvéd's passing game, the visitors might struggle to be as effective. The boss asked club staff and apprentices to water the pitch as best they could during the break – and the tactic immediately paid off as Johnny Hancocks reduced the arrears 4 minutes after the restart from the penalty spot.

Wolves gradually took control of the game and on 76 minutes, Roy Swinbourne finally levelled the scores and 2 minutes later, Molineux was in raptures as Swinbourne finished a fine move to make it 3-2. While Wolves played a long-ball game, the Hungarians struggled to cope with the boggy conditions that were making their style of play difficult, to say the least. Honvéd couldn't find an equaliser and Wolves held on for a famous win.

Cullis didn't underplay the result to waiting media afterwards, instead claiming his side were 'champions of the world'. Wolves had restored national pride in beating Honvéd, but received criticism from some quarters, most notably international writers, that the watering tactics were the real reason Wolves had won and that Cullis' team were inferior to Real Madrid and AC Milan. One journalist suggested a competition should be organised to find out who the best team really was and the idea struck a chord not only with the general public but the football authorities as well. The following year saw the European Cup launched for the first time.

Cullis, while welcoming the challenge, claimed,

> The whole future of football in Britain depends on our ability to face the challenge from abroad. Although I am in a minority, I am sure we would be wise to screen more games live. Television offers an opportunity not seen in all soccer's history, a whole new source of revenue, a vast sum which must make a considerable impact on the game.

How right he was and, looking back, what a landmark game the Wolves *v*. Honvéd match proved to be.

SCOTLAND THE BRAVE

Here are a couple Wolves favourites and their history for the Tartan Army – random, but interesting.

Andy Gray (1975–83)

Caps: 20
Goals: 7

Despite a more than useful record at club level, Andy Gray's international career never really took off. He won an average of two caps a year following his 1975 debut against Romania and managed seven goals during a decade of football for his country. Ask any Dundee, Aston Villa, Wolves or Everton fan why Gray didn't win double the amount of caps he actually did, and chances are they will be lost for an answer. Gray, a typical old-fashioned centre forward, hard as nails and lethal in the air, did have the likes of Joe Jordan and Kenny Dalglish blocking his path, it's true, but for some reason he could never win a regular starting place in the squad, regardless of his scoring feats for a succession of club sides. He was never selected to play in either the 1974, 1978, 1982 or 1986 World Cup finals and it's hard to imagine that he doesn't look back with some wonderment as to why that was. Gray moved into a successful career in the media following his retirement and is now among the best-paid and respected football commentators on British TV, with his phrases 'Right on cue' and 'Take a bow son' now part of the British football language.

Kenny Miller (2001–present)

Caps: 69
Goals: 18

Not unlike James McFadden, Kenny Miller should take his place within the Scotland Hall of Fame within the next few years. Something of a nomadic player at club level, the Edinburgh-born striker has played for six different teams, including Hibs, Rangers, Celtic, Wolves and Derby County – the latter being his current home. After picking up the Scottish Young Player of the Year award in 2000 while with Hibs, Miller moved on to Rangers for £2 million and towards the end of his first season at Ibrox, he made his international debut against Poland. He has been a regular for his country since then, sometimes playing as part of a front pairing, sometimes as a lone striker. His energetic, wholehearted attitude has ensured he has retained his place under three different Scotland managers and his 10-goal haul represents a decent return from his 35 caps. He has been booked in four internationals – and scored in each game where he was cautioned – clearly, the passion burns brightly for Miller every time he pulls on the navy-blue jersey.

GEORGIAN DRAGON

Georgian forward Timouri Ketsbaia enjoyed a fruitful career with Dinamo Tbilisi before moving to Cyprus and eventually Newcastle United where he became a cult figure during his three years on Tyneside. He famously scored a late winner at Bolton where he celebrated by kicking ten shades of you know what out of an advertising hoardings as he vented his frustration at not playing more regularly. Ketsbaia joined Wolves in 2000 for £900,000 as a replacement for Leicester City-bound Ade Akinbiyi. Speaking of his move at the time, he said, 'I'm very happy to be signing for Wolves. I can see Wolves have ambition to be in the Premier League. I hope for the fans we can do that this season.'

Timouri, known for being a player who wore his heart on his sleeve, made a terrific start to life at Molineux when he scored a long-range cracker in the 1-1 draw with Sheffield Wednesday. His time in the Black Country was to be brief, however, as he made just 24 appearances and scored three goals before shipping out to Dundee just over a year later. He retired in 2007 and moved into management with Anorthosis and was then appointed Olympiacos boss in 2009, leaving the post after just four months in charge. Ketsbaia was then given the role of managing Georgia a month later and held the post for five years before resigning after a 4-0 defeat to Poland.

HI HO WOLVERHAMPTON!

The popular chant in short form, but here are the full lyrics – not that popular with supporters, many of whom claim the words to be embarrassing!

We're Wolverhampton Wanderers baby,
Remember times of old,
Billy Wright and Stevie Bull,
Scoring loads of goals,
But now the tide and times are changing,
We're gonna get it right,
Now get up on your feet and sing it,
Until the morning light!
Cause it's Hi Ho Wolverhampton,
Let's score some goals, now baby,
You'll see the good times coming,
We'll be on a roll,
Cause we're the Wanderers!

We're Wolverhampton Wanderers baby,
We're wearing gold and black,
We're gonna take the game right to ya,

An all out attack,
We need you all to get behind us,
And cheer us on,
So stand up tall and raise your voices,
And sing on and on!

Cause it's Hi Ho Wolverhampton,
Let's score some goals, now baby,
You'll see the good times coming,
We'll be on a roll,
Cause we're the Wanderers!

We're Wolverhampton Wanderers baby,
Who the hell are you?
We're gonna take the game right to ya,
Nothing you can do,
So get back on your bus and go home,
The three points are ours,
Now get up on your feet and sing it,
And sing it proud!

Cause it's Hi Ho Wolverhampton,
Let's score some goals, now baby,
You'll see the good times coming,
We'll be on a roll,
Cause we're the Wanderers!

SEOUL MAN

South Korean striker Seol Ki-Hyeon spent a couple of seasons with Wolves, making 69 appearances and scoring eight goals between 2004 and 2006. He would win 82 caps for his country during a distinguished career, but his goal against Crystal Palace on 10 December 2005 made sure his name would be etched into club history as it was Wolves' 7,000th League goal – the Gold and Blacks were the first to reach the milestone and Seol, while perhaps not a club legend, can tell his grandchildren he made his mark on English football.

ACCRINGTON STANLEY – WHO ARE THEY?

One of the best named football clubs in English football are also steeped in history and have met Wolves on a number of occasions. One thing is for sure – when these two teams get together, there's always plenty of goals. Accrington and Wolves have met 15 times to date, stretching back 127 years. The first meeting set the tone of what was to come with a 4-4 draw in Lancashire in 1888. Wolves won the return 4-0 and then the next game in the Black Country 2-1. Accrington recorded their first win that same season with a 6-3 victory, meaning 29 goals had been scored in this fixture in just four matches – more than seven per meeting up to that point. Wolves won the next four meetings between 1890 and 1891 and it was in the 1891 Molineux fixture that Wolves were awarded the first ever penalty in League football. Joseph Heath converted the spot-kick to write his name the history books – and this one – and Wolves went on to win 5-0. Accrington won two of the next three meetings. Accrington joined the Football League in 1921 and the teams met again in the 1923/24 campaign, with Accrington winning the first meeting 1-0 and then Wolves winning the return 5-1 a week later. Accrington disappeared as a club in 1966 and it was 1970 before it reformed. The teams then didn't meet again until 2008, some 85 years later and the scoring continued with Wolves edging a Carling Cup tie 3-2 at Molineux. The 14 meetings to date have yielded 67 goals – almost an average of five goals per game!

The total record is as follows:

Played: 14
Won: 9
Drawn: 1
Lost: 4
For: 41
Against: 26

BERRY DISTINCT!

Former Wolves centre-back George Berry had one of the first afro hairstyles ever worn by a top division footballer in England. Berry, who wore gold and black between 1976 and 1982, made 124 appearances and scored four goals. Berry was born in Germany where his Jamaican father was a serviceman. Berry's mum was from Wales, making the defender a truly international footballer. Voted the club's Player of the Year in 1979, Berry was an uncompromising figure who was prepared to deal with bigots in his own unique way. After being racially abused one time, Berry said,

> We had just lost 3–0 at home to Watford in the FA cup and some bloke shouted abuse at me and I just lost it and jumped into the crowd and started to beat him up. We went to the police station and I got a bollocking from the chief inspector, but it all got hushed up.

Nobody messed with George, who left for Stoke City and later played for Doncaster, Aldershot, Preston North End, Peterborough United and Stafford Rangers.

YOU'RE BARD!

Of all the FA Cup ties Wolves have been involved with over the years, nobody comes close to beating Aston Shakespeare for the best-named opposition. Wolves won the tie 3-0 and never played the non-League side, who disappeared into the ether shortly after.

ROCKIN' ROBINS

Famed north-west cup giant-killers Altrincham first made the FA Cup first round in 1934 when they were beaten by Gainsborough Trinity. It would be another 30 years before they made it to the first round again, drawing with Wrexham before losing the replay. Two years later, the Robins finally beat Scarborough – by 6-0 no less – to progress to the second round where they then beat Rochdale 3-1 at Spotland. In with the big boys, Altrincham pulled second division Wolves out of the hat for the third round and a money-spinning tie at Molineux where more than 30,000 watched the Gold and Blacks triumph 5-0. Wolves went on to reach the fifth round where Manchester United ended dreams of Wembley with a 4-2 victory at Molineux, with the Reds dipping out in the semi-final against Everton.

THESE COLOURS DON'T RUN

The most distinctive kit in English football, the association of 'old gold' and black is said to relate to the city council's motto 'Out of the darkness cometh light'. Wolves, who began life as St Luke's, wore colours more akin to Stoke City than the future Wolverhampton Wanderers. When Wolves did adopt their new colours, a mix of stripes and diagonal halves were initially used before the plain gold shirt and black shorts were used from the 1930s onwards, though a darker shade of gold was used until the 1960s.

STAN CULLIS – IRON MANAGER

The words and wisdom of one of Wolverhampton Wanderers' greatest managers of all time.

I want us to see eye to eye from the start. I want, and I am going to get, one hundred per cent effort out of all of you, both on and off the field. If I can get this support, you can take it from me I will be one hundred per cent behind you. Nothing else is going to be enough.

Cullis addresses the squad shortly after taking control in 1948.

I cannot stress too often that the three great virtues of soccer are spirit, tactics and fitness – and the greatest of these might easily be fitness. People used to say that I was an iron man manager, but I had a principle that the players were representing the town of Wolverhampton Wanderers. It was their duty to acknowledge that and for that reason, they had to work hard. I'm sure our training schedule was as hard as anyone's in the country – and it paid off.

Cullis reveals the secrets behind his management.

There is no substitute for hard work – put that sign up above the dressing room of every club in the land and we will get soccer back on the road to recovery. I remember the astounded look on the face of one League manager when I told him my boys came back in the afternoon for more training. I might as well have told him I'd set the boardroom on fire.

Cullis – no shirkers allowed on his shift!

I thought I could never be more proud of them than when they beat Spartak, but tonight has surpassed everything. The second half was the greatest performance I have ever seen.

Cullis – proud of Wolves' epic and historic victory over Honved.

JOHN RICHARDS – GOLD-AND-BLACK LEGEND

I went down to Molineux on the following Sunday morning and remember how impressed I was by all the trophies in the cabinet and the foyer. Wolverhampton Wanderers were still one of the biggest clubs in the country and I found the place very awe-inspiring.

Richards on his first impressions of the club, 1969.

One of the most prolific strikers Wolves have ever had, John Richards' 194 goals in 486 appearances makes him a club great – here are some of his best quotes.

The big disappointment was that we were up against Tottenham in the final. Playing another English side was an anti-climax and there wasn't that much interest considering it was a European final. We lost 2-1 at home and drew 1-1 away but it had still been a great experience.

Richards on the 1971/72 UEFA Cup final.

The Christians had a better chance with the Romans than I've had a Molineux this year!

Richards, 1983 – towards the end of his time at the club.

MERCANTILE CREDIT

Wolves took part in a Centenary League competition at Wembley in April 1988. One of those half-baked ideas that hold little interest to the paying fans, Wolves entered at the second phase and took on Everton, drawing 1-1 before losing 3-2 on penalties. Just 21,446 bothered to turn up with Robbie Dennison scoring Wolves' only goal.

MAKING A MELIA OUT OF IT

Jimmy Melia didn't make a massive impression during his time with Wolves, making just 24 appearances and finding the net four times in the mid-1960s. He made his name with his home city club Liverpool and later went into management, taking Brighton & Hove Albion to the 1983 FA Cup final where they were beaten 4-0 by Manchester United – despite Jimmy's lucky white shoes!

NUMBER'S UP

Wolves players are believed to have worn shirt numbers for the first time when they took on Stoke City in a Jubilee Fund Game in August 1938. The Nos 2–11 jerseys made it easier for fans to identify their heroes – especially on some of the mud-covered bogs that were a sorry excuse for pitches back then.

SOMETHING IN RESERVE

The first recorded Wolverhampton Wanderers reserve team match was on 15 November 1884 when 'the Stiffs' beat Astbury 10-1 in the Birmingham Junior Cup. Wolves reached the semi-final of the competition before losing 2-1 to Bilston at Perry Bar.

WOLVES' ALL-TIME LEAGUE RECORD

In this fascinating table, the complete record of all 141 clubs who have taken part in English League football, Wolves lie in a magnificent fifth overall as of 1 October 2014 – that's higher than Chelsea, Spurs, Everton, Manchester City and Aston Villa, to name but a few. City have scored 7,486 goals at the time of writing, conceding 617 goals less. A strong League campaign in 2014/15 could see Wolves leap up to fourth with Preston only one victory ahead when the table was compiled.

		Home					Away					
		P	W	D	L	F	A	W	D	L	F	A	Pt
1	Man U	4410	1352	479	374	4496	2078	765	570	870	3162	3518	6036
2	Liverpool	4378	1348	489	352	4599	2129	726	576	887	2888	3253	5890
3	Arsenal	4378	1295	516	378	4429	2127	704	579	906	2911	3402	5767

4	Preston NE	4739	1256	602	512	4374	2662	581	603	1185	2678	4005	5458
5	Wolves	4679	1271	540	528	4576	2653	619	568	1153	2910	4216	5455
6	Sheff U	4593	1223	582	491	4257	2538	612	558	1127	2763	4056	5405
7	Everton	4502	1239	549	463	4409	2491	608	580	1063	2711	3783	5340
8	Burnley	4712	1250	580	526	4304	2609	568	572	1216	2630	4298	5339
9	Man C	4452	1252	490	484	4452	2526	583	582	1061	2798	3844	5293
10	Aston V	4514	1249	521	487	4468	2540	614	564	1079	2842	3976	5281

(Courtesy of Statto.com)

ALL-TIME FA CUP TABLE

Wolves FA Cup record leaves a bit more to be desired, lying 17th out of 250. Here is the complete record (with three points for a win for table purposes) – and the teams that lie above:

		P	W	D	L	F	A	Pt
1	Man Utd	420	227	96	97	760	472	777
2	Arsenal	429	227	102	100	729	445	783
3	Everton	416	224	82	110	757	465	754
4	Liverpool	412	217	91	104	682	393	742
5	Chelsea	378	196	91	91	680	401	679
6	Tottenham Hotspur	398	201	99	98	767	479	702
7	Aston Villa	409	212	80	117	832	527	716
8	Man City	337	165	69	103	607	424	564
9	Blackburn Rovers	394	191	86	117	733	466	659
10	Peterborough United	215	103	48	64	375	292	357
11	West Brom Albion	382	184	82	116	672	454	634
12	Newcastle United	359	170	85	104	623	445	595
13	Bolton Wanderers	385	179	90	116	650	502	627
14	Sheffield Weds	392	181	94	117	692	497	637
15	Swindon Town	290	140	50	100	509	400	470
16	Preston NE	346	164	65	117	663	450	557
17	Wolves	372	170	85	117	661	475	595
18	Sheffield Utd	360	161	89	110	533	439	572
19	Darwen	63	30	8	25	157	117	98
20	Derby County	332	151	62	119	605	513	515

(Courtesy of Statto.com)

ALL-TIME LEAGUE CUP RECORD

Wolves' least successful domestic cup competition is the League Cup, failing to win 87 of the 135 ties played to date. Lying in 35th, it's clear the club don't enjoy this competition as much as the League and FA Cup! The Top 35 teams are below.

		P	W	D	L	F	A	Pt
1	Liverpool	217	125	50	42	438	213	425
2	Tottenham Hotspur	201	119	34	48	394	212	391
3	Aston Villa	232	135	44	53	457	271	449
4	Arsenal	215	120	46	49	397	215	406
5	Man Utd	184	105	29	50	324	207	344
6	Man City	198	105	38	55	381	228	353
7	Nottingham Forest	192	98	44	50	367	223	338
8	West Ham United	208	108	40	60	385	258	364
9	Norwich City	202	103	42	57	345	237	351
10	Chelsea	185	93	41	51	335	223	320
11	Sheffield Weds	168	81	36	51	281	217	279
12	Southampton	188	89	45	54	326	224	312
13	Everton	167	79	40	48	300	183	277
14	Leicester City	172	85	30	57	287	232	285
15	QPR	166	82	27	57	302	218	273
16	MK Dons	25	13	2	10	47	43	41
17	Ipswich Town	168	81	31	56	282	228	274
18	Coventry City	160	79	22	59	274	238	259
19	Leeds United	174	85	25	64	292	232	280
20	Birmingham City	194	90	42	62	321	264	312
21	West Brom Albion	168	77	39	52	275	223	270
22	Blackburn Rovers	173	80	37	56	304	238	277
23	Crystal Palace	185	83	42	60	287	233	291

		P	W	D	L	F	A	Pt
24	Middlesbrough	172	77	37	58	260	196	268
25	Bolton Wanderers	182	82	37	63	300	282	283
26	Oxford United	160	69	38	53	230	205	245
27	Sheffield Utd	158	70	31	57	248	223	241
28	Swindon Town	179	78	38	63	292	266	272
29	Sunderland	163	71	34	58	265	231	247
30	Wimbledon	99	42	24	33	147	126	150
31	Stoke City	169	71	42	56	241	228	255
32	Newcastle United	135	61	19	55	216	188	202
33	Burnley	174	75	33	66	276	257	258
34	Watford	172	73	35	64	271	241	254
35	**Wolves**	135	58	25	52	214	190	199

(*Courtesy of Statto.com*)

OTHER CUPS/COMPETITION HONOURS

Not all trophies won have been major domestic honours – but each cup/shield or whatever won is worth a mention and we present here a list of so-called lesser lights that all meant something at some point.

Football League Trophy: Winners – 1988
Texaco Cup: Winners – 1971
Football League War Cup: Winners – 1942
FA Youth Cup: Winners – 1958
FA Youth Cup: Runners-up – 1953, 1954, 1962, 1976
United Soccer Association: Champions – 1967 (playing as Los Angeles Wolves)
NASL International Cup: Winners – 1969 (playing as Kansas City Spurs)
The Central League (reserve division): Winners – 1931/32, 1950/51, 1951/52, 1952/53, 1957/58, 1958/59
Birmingham Senior Cup: Winners – 1891/92, 1892/93, 1893/94, 1899/1900, 1901/02, 1923/24, 1986/87
Birmingham Senior Cup: Runners-up – 1888/89, 1896/97, 1897/98, 1903/04, 1906/07, 1908/09, 1912/13, 1998/99, 2003/04

Birmingham Football Combination: Winners – 1934/35
Birmingham & District League: Winners – 1892/93, 1897/98, 1898/99, 1900/01, 1953/54, 1957/58, 1958/59
Worcestershire Football Combination: Winners – 1957/58
Staffordshire Senior Cup: Winners – 1887/88, 1893/94, 1966/67
Staffordshire Senior Cup: Runners-up – 1884/85
Walsall Senior Cup: Runners-up – 1885/86
Wrekin Cup: Winners – 1884 (First trophy won by the club)
Gothia World Youth Cup: Winners – 2009

WOLVES' RECORDS AND STATISTICS – IN BRIEF FOR EASY REFERENCE

Firsts

First known match: St Luke's 0-8 Stafford Road, 13 January 1877
First FA Cup match: Wolves 4-1 Long Eaton Rangers, first round, 27 October 1883
First Football League match: Wolves 1-1 Aston Villa, 8 September 1888
First match at Molineux: Wolves 1-0 Aston Villa, friendly, 2 September 1889
First European match: Wolves 2-2 Schalke, European Cup second round first leg, 12 November 1958
First League Cup match: Wolves 2-1 Mansfield Town, second round, 13 September 1966

Record Wins

Record win: Wolves 14-0 Crosswell's Brewery, FA Cup second round, 13 November 1886
Record League win: Wolves 10-1 Leicester City, Division One, 15 April 1938
Record FA Cup win: Wolves 14-0 Crosswell's Brewery, FA Cup second round, 13 November 1886
Record League Cup win: Wolves 6-1 Shrewsbury Town, second round first leg, 24 September 1991
Record European win: Wolves 5-0 Austria Vienna, European Cup Winners' Cup quarter-final second leg, 30 November 1960
Record home win (League): Wolves 10-1 Leicester City, Division One, 15 April 1938

Record home win (cup): Wolves 14-0 Crosswell's Brewery, FA Cup second round, 13 November 1886
Record away win (League): Wolves 9-1 Cardiff City, Division One, 3 September 1955
Record away win (cup): Wolves 5-0 Grimsby Town, FA Cup semi-final, 25 March 1939 (neutral venue)

Record Defeats

Record defeat: Wolves 1-10 Newton Heath, Division One, 15 October 1892
Record League defeat: Wolves 1-10 Newton Heath, Division One, 15 October 1892
Record FA Cup defeat: Wolves 0-6 Rotherham United, first round, 16 November 1985
Record League Cup defeat: Wolves 0-6 Chelsea, third round, 25 September 2012
Record European defeat: Wolves 0-4 Barcelona, European Cup second round first leg, 10 February 1960
Record home defeat (League): Wolves 0-8 West Bromwich Albion, Division One, 27 December 1897
Record home defeat (cup): Wolves 3-6 Derby County, FA Cup third round, 14 January 1933
Record away defeat (League): Wolves 1-10 Newton Heath, Division One, 15 October 1892
Record away defeat (cup): Wolves 0-6 Rotherham United, FA Cup first round, 16 November 1985; and Wolves 0-6 Chelsea; League Cup third round, 25 September 2012

Streaks (League Games Only)

Longest unbeaten run: 21 games (January–August 2005)
Longest unbeaten run in home games: 27 games (March 1923–September 1924)
Longest unbeaten run in away games: 11 games (September 1953–January 1954)
Longest winning run: 9 games (January–March 2014)
Longest winning run in home games: 14 games (March–December 1953)
Longest winning run in away games: 5 games (during 1938, 1962, 1980, 2001, 2013)
Longest winless run: 19 games (December 1984–April 1985)

Longest winless run in home games: 13 games (November 1984–May 1985)

Longest winless run in away games: 32 games (March 1922–October 1923)

Longest scoring run: 41 games (December 1958–December 1959)

Longest scoreless run: 7 games (February–March 1985)

Longest run of clean sheets: 8 games (August–October 1982)

Longest run without a clean sheet: 30 games (September 2011–April 2012)

Goals

Most League goals scored in a season: 115 (Division Two; 1931/32)

Fewest League goals scored in a season: 27 (Division One; 1983/84)

Most League goals conceded in a season: 99 (Division One; 1905/06)

Fewest League goals conceded in a season: 27 (Division Three; 1923/24)

Most goals scored in a game (League): 10 (*v.* Leicester City, Division One, 15 April 1938)

Most goals scored in a game (cup): 14 (*v.* Crosswell's Brewery, FA Cup second round, 13 November 1886)

Points

Most points in a season:

Two points for a win: 64 (Division One, 1957/58)

Three points for a win: 103 (League One, 2013/14)

Fewest points in a season:

Two points for a win: 21 (Division One, 1895/96)

Three points for a win: 25 (Premier League, 2011/12)

Attendances

Highest home attendance: 61,315 *v.* Liverpool, FA Cup fourth round, 11 February 1939

Highest League attendance: 58,661 *v.* West Bromwich Albion, Division One, 15 October 1949

Highest average League attendance: 45,346 (1949/50 season)

Season-by-Season Performance (Miscellaneous Feats)

Wolves were awarded, and scored from, the Football League's first ever penalty kick on 14 September 1891.

Wolves were the first (and, as of 2014, the only) English League team to pass the 100-goal mark for four seasons in succession, in the 1957/58, 1958/59, 1959/60 and 1960/61 seasons.

In 2005, Wolves became the first team to have scored 7,000 League goals and currently trail only Manchester United in terms of total League goals (as of the end of the 2012/13 season).

(*Source: Wikipedia*)

WOLVERHAMPTON WANDERERS TIMELINE

1888/89	Founder member of Football League
	FA Cup runners-up
1889/90	FA Cup semi-finalists
1892/93	FA Cup winners
1895/96	FA Cup runners-up
1906	Relegated to Division Two
1907/08	FA Cup winners (2nd time)
1920/21	FA Cup runners-up
1923	Relegated to Division Three North
1923/24	Football League Division Three North champions
	Promoted to Division Two
1931/32	Football League Division Two champions
	Promoted to Division One
1937/38	Football League runners-up
1938/39	Football League runners-up
	FA Cup runners-up
1939/40	Football League programme abandoned due to outbreak of war
1946/47	Missed runners-up spot on goal average
1948/49	FA Cup winners (3rd time)
1949/50	Football League runners-up (lost title on goal average)
1950/51	FA Cup semi-finalists
1953/54	Football League champions
1954/55	Football League runners-up

1955/56	Missed Football League runners-up spot on goal average
1957/58	Football League champions (2nd time)
1958/59	Football League champions (3rd time)
1959/60	Football League runners-up
	European Cup quarter-finalists
	FA Cup Winners (4th time)
1960/61	European Cup Winners Cup semi-finalists
1965	Relegated to Division Two
1966/67	Football League Division Two runners-up
	Promoted to Division One
1971/72	UEFA Cup runners-up
1972/73	Football League Cup semi-finalists
	FA Cup semi-finalists
1973/74	Football League Cup winners
1976	Relegated to Division Two
1976/77	Football League Division Two champions
	Promoted to Division One
1978/79	FA Cup semi-finalists
1979/80	Football League Cup winners (2nd time)
1980/81	FA Cup semi-finalists
1982	Relegated to Division Two
1982/83	Football League Division Two runners-up
	Promoted to Division One
1984	Relegated to Division Two
1985	Relegated to Division Three
1986	Relegated to Division Four
1986/87	Not promoted after play-offs
	First leg: Colchester United 0-2 Wolverhampton Wanderers
	Second leg: Wolverhampton Wanderers 0-0 Colchester United (Agg. 2-0)
	Final first leg: Aldershot 2-0 Wolverhampton Wanderers
	Final second leg: Wolverhampton Wanderers 0-1 Aldershot (Agg. 0-3)
1987/88	Football League Division Four champions
	Promoted to Division Three
1988/89	Football League Division Three Champions
	Promoted to Division Two
1992/93	Division Two redesignated Division One on formation of FA Premier League
1994/95	Not promoted after play-offs
	Semi-final first leg: Wolverhampton Wanderers 2-1 Bolton Wanderers

	Semi-final second leg: Bolton Wanderers 2-0 Wolverhampton Wanderers (Agg. 2-3)

Semi-final second leg: Bolton Wanderers 2-0 Wolverhampton Wanderers (Agg. 2-3)

1996/97 Not promoted after play-offs
Semi-final first leg: Crystal Palace 3-1 Wolverhampton Wanderers
Semi-final second leg: Wolverhampton Wanderers 2-1 Crystal Palace (Agg. 3-4)

1997/98 FA Cup semi-finalists

2001/02 Not promoted after play-offs
Semi-final first leg: Norwich City 3-1 Wolverhampton Wanderers
Semi-final second leg: Wolverhampton Wanderers 1-0 Norwich City (Agg. 2-3)

2002/03 Promoted to FA Premier League after play-offs
Semi-final first leg: Wolverhampton Wanderers 2-1 Reading
Semi-final second leg: Reading 0-1 Wolverhampton Wanderers (Agg. 3-1)
Final: Sheffield United 0-3 Wolverhampton Wanderers (at Millennium Stadium, Cardiff)

2004 Relegated to Division One, then renamed Football League Championship

2006/07 Not promoted after play-offs
Semi-final first leg: Wolverhampton Wanderers 2-3 West Bromwich Albion
Semi-final second leg: West Bromwich Albion 1-0 Wolverhampton Wanderers (Agg. 2-4)

2008/09 Football League Champions (fourth time)
Promoted to FA Premier League

2012 Relegated to Football League Championship

2013 Relegated to League One

2013/14 Football League One Champions

(Courtesy of F. C. H. D –The Football Club History Database)

WOLVES' COMPLETE LEAGUE HISTORY

Season	League	P	W	D	L	F	A	P	Season	League	P	W	D	L	F	A	P
1888/89	FL	22	12	4	6	50	37	28	1898/99	FL-1	34	14	7	13	54	48	35
1889/90	FL	22	10	5	7	51	38	25	1899/1900	FL-1	34	15	9	10	48	37	39
1890/91	FL	22	12	2	8	39	50	26	1900/01	FL-1	34	9	13	12	39	55	31
1891/92	FL	26	11	4	11	59	46	26	1901/02	FL-1	34	13	6	15	46	57	32
1892/93	FL-1	30	12	4	14	47	68	28	1902/03	FL-1	34	14	5	15	48	57	33
1893/94	FL-1	30	14	3	13	52	63	31	1903/04	FL-1	34	14	8	12	44	66	36
1894/95	FL-1	30	9	7	14	43	63	25	1904/05	FL-1	34	11	4	19	47	73	26
1895/96	FL-1	30	10	1	19	61	65	21	1905/06	FL-1	38	8	7	23	58	99	23
1896/97	FL-1	30	11	6	13	45	41	28	1906/07	FL-2	38	17	7	14	66	53	41
1897/98	FL-1	30	14	7	9	57	41	35	1907/08	FL-2	38	15	7	16	50	45	37

Season	League	P	W	D	L	F	A	P	Season	League	P	W	D	L	F	A	P
1908/09	FL-2	38	14	11	13	56	48	39	1966/67	FL-2	42	25	8	9	88	48	58
1909/10	FL-2	38	17	6	15	64	63	40	1967/68	FL-1	42	14	8	20	66	75	36
1910/11	FL-2	38	15	8	15	51	52	38	1968/69	FL-1	42	10	15	17	41	58	35
1911/12	FL-2	38	16	10	12	57	33	42	1969/70	FL-1	42	12	16	14	55	57	40
1912/13	FL-2	38	14	10	14	56	54	38	1970/71	FL-1	42	22	8	12	64	54	52
1913/14	FL-2	38	18	5	15	51	52	41	1971/72	FL-1	42	18	11	13	65	57	47
1914/15	FL-2	38	19	7	12	77	52	45	1972/73	FL-1	42	18	11	13	66	54	47
1919/20	FL-2	42	10	10	22	55	80	30	1973/74	FL-1	42	13	15	14	49	49	41
1920/21	FL-2	42	16	6	20	49	66	38	1974/75	FL-1	42	14	11	17	57	54	39
1921/22	FL-2	42	13	11	18	44	49	37	1975/76	FL-1	42	10	10	22	51	68	30
1922/23	FL-2	42	9	9	24	42	77	27	1976/77	FL-2	42	22	13	7	84	45	57
1923/24	FL-3N	42	24	15	3	76	27	63	1977/78	FL-1	42	12	12	18	51	64	36
1924/25	FL-2	42	20	6	16	55	51	46	1978/79	FL-1	42	13	8	21	44	68	34
1925/26	FL-2	42	21	7	14	84	60	49	1979/80	FL-1	42	19	9	14	58	47	47
1926/27	FL-2	42	14	7	21	73	75	35	1980/81	FL-1	42	13	9	20	43	55	35
1927/28	FL-2	42	13	10	19	63	91	36	1981/82	FL-1	42	10	10	22	32	63	40
1928/29	FL-2	42	15	7	20	77	81	37	1982/83	FL-2	42	20	15	7	68	44	75
1929/30	FL-2	42	16	9	17	77	79	41	1983/84	FL-1	42	6	11	25	27	80	29
1930/31	FL-2	42	21	5	16	84	67	47	1984/85	FL-2	42	8	9	25	37	79	33
1931/32	FL-2	42	24	8	10	115	49	56	1985/86	FL-3	46	11	10	25	57	98	43
1932/33	FL-1	42	13	9	20	80	96	35	1986/87	FL-4	46	24	7	15	69	50	79
1933/34	FL-1	42	14	12	16	74	86	40	1987/88	FL-4	46	27	9	10	82	43	90
1934/35	FL-1	42	15	8	19	88	94	38	1988/89	FL-3	46	26	14	6	96	49	92
1935/36	FL-1	42	15	10	17	77	76	40	1989/90	FL-2	46	18	13	15	67	60	67
1936/37	FL-1	42	21	5	16	84	67	47	1990/91	FL-2	46	13	19	14	63	63	58
1937/38	FL-1	42	20	11	11	72	49	51	1991/92	FL-2	46	18	10	18	61	54	64
1938/39	FL-1	42	22	11	9	88	39	55	1992/93	FL-1	46	16	13	17	57	56	61
1939/40	FL-1	3	0	2	1	3	4	2	1993/94	FL-1	46	17	17	12	60	47	68
1946/47	FL-1	42	25	6	11	98	56	56	1994/95	FL-1	46	21	13	12	77	61	76
1947/48	FL-1	42	19	9	14	83	70	47	1995/96	FL-1	46	13	16	17	56	62	55
1948/49	FL-1	42	17	12	13	79	66	46	1996/97	FL-1	46	22	10	14	68	51	76
1949/50	FL-1	42	20	13	9	76	49	53	1997/98	FL-1	46	18	11	17	57	53	65
1950/51	FL-1	42	15	8	19	74	61	38	1998/99	FL-1	46	19	16	11	64	43	73
1951/52	FL-1	42	12	14	16	73	73	38	1999/2000	FL-1	46	21	11	14	64	48	74
1952/53	FL-1	42	19	13	10	86	63	51	2000/01	FL-1	46	14	13	19	45	48	55
1953/54	FL-1	42	25	7	10	96	56	57	2001/02	FL-1	46	25	11	10	76	43	86
1954/55	FL-1	42	19	10	13	89	70	48	2002/03	FL-1	46	20	16	10	81	44	76
1955/56	FL-1	42	20	9	13	89	65	49	2003/04	FA-PREM	38	7	12	19	33	38	77
1956/57	FL-1	42	20	8	14	94	70	48	2004/05	FL-CH	46	15	21	10	72	59	66
1957/58	FL-1	42	28	8	6	103	47	64	2005/06	FL-CH	46	16	19	11	50	42	67
1958/59	FL-1	42	28	5	9	110	49	61	2006/07	FL-CH	46	22	10	14	59	56	76
1959/60	FL-1	42	24	6	12	106	67	54	2007/08	FL-CH	46	18	16	12	53	48	70
1960/61	FL-1	42	25	7	10	103	75	57	2008/09	FL-CH	46	27	9	10	80	52	90
1961/62	FL-1	42	13	10	19	73	86	36	2009/10	FA-PREM	38	9	11	18	32	56	38
1962/63	FL-1	42	20	10	12	93	65	50	2010/11	FA-PREM	38	11	7	20	46	66	40
1963/64	FL-1	42	12	15	15	70	80	39	2011/12	FA-PREM	38	5	10	23	40	82	25
1964/65	FL-1	42	13	4	25	59	89	30	2012/13	FL-CH	46	14	9	23	55	69	51
1965/66	FL-2	42	20	10	12	87	61	50	2013/14	FL-1	46	31	10	5	89	31	103

(Courtesy of F. C. H. D – The Football Club History Database)

WOLVES IN EUROPE

Here is Wolves' complete record in Europe to date.

SEASON	CUP	RD	OPPONENTS		VEN	SCORE
1958/59	EC	PRE	BYE			
		1	Schalke 04 (GER)		H	2-2
			Schalke 04 (GER)		A	1-2 (Agg. 3-4)
1959/60	EC	PRE	Vorwärts (GDR)		A	1-2
			Vorwärts (GDR)		H	2-0 (Agg 3-2)
		1	Crvena Zvezda (YUG)		A	1-1
			Crvena Zvezda (YUG)		H	3-0 (Agg 4-1)
		QF	Barcelona (ESP)		A	0-4
			Barcelona (ESP)		H	2-5 (Agg 2-9)
1960/61	CWC	QF	Austria Vienna (AUT)		A	0-2
			Austria Vienna (AUT)		H	5-0 (Agg 5-2)
		SF	Rangers (SCO)		A	0-2
			Rangers (SCO)		H	1-1 (Agg 1-3)
1971/72		1	Academica Coimbra (POR)		H	3-0
			Academica Coimbra (POR)		A	4-1 (Agg 7-1)
		2	Den Haag (NED)		A	3-1
			Den Haag (NED)		H	4-0 (Agg 7-1)
		3	Carl Zeiss Jena (GDR)		A	1-0
			Carl Zeiss Jena (GDR)		H	3-0 (Agg 4-0)
		QF	Juventus (ITA)		A	1-1
			Juventus (ITA)		H	2-1 (Agg 3-2)
		SF	Ferencvárosi (HUN)		A	2-2
			Ferencvárosi (HUN)		H	2-1 (Agg 4-3)
		F	Tottenham Hotspur (ENG)		H	1-2
			Tottenham Hotspur (ENG)		A	1-1 (Agg 2-3)
1973/74	UEFA	1	Belenenses (POR)		A	2-0
			Belenenses (POR)		H	2-1 (Agg 4-1)
		2	Lokomotiv Leipzig (GDR)		A	0-3
			Lokomotiv Leipzig (GDR)		A	4-1 (Agg 4-4)
			Wolverhampton Wanderers lost on away goals			
1974/75	UEFA	1	Porto (POR)		A	1-4
			Porto (POR)		H	3-1 (Agg 4-5)
1980/81	UEFA	1	PSV Eindhoven (NED)		A	1-3
			PSV Eindhoven (NED)		H	1-0 (Agg 2-3)

(*Courtesy of F. C. H. D. – The Football Club History Database*)

FA CUP COMPLETE HISTORY

SEASON	RD	OPPONENTS	VEN	SCORE	
1885/86	3	Walsall Swifts	H	2-1	
	4	West Bromwich Albion	A	1-3	
1886/87	3	Aston Villa	A	2-2	
	3r	Aston Villa	H	1-1	
	3r2	Aston Villa	H	3-3	
	3r3	Aston Villa	A	0-2	
1887/88	3	West Bromwich Albion	A	0-2	
1888/89	1	Old Carthusians	H	4-3	
	2	Walsall Town Swifts	H	6-1	
	QF	Sheffield Wednesday	H	3-0	
	SF	Blackburn Rovers	N	1-1	At Crewe Alexandra
	SFr	Blackburn Rovers	N	3-1	At Crewe Alexandra
	F	Preston North End	N	0-3	At Kennington Oval
1889/90	1	Old Carthusians	H	2-0	
	2	Small Heath	H	2-1	
	QF	Stoke	H	4-0	Declared void
	QF	Stoke	H	8-0	
	SF	Blackburn Rovers	N	0-1	At Racecourse Ground, Derby
1890/91	1	Long Eaton Rangers	A	2-1	
	2	Accrington	A	3-2	
	QF	Blackburn Rovers	A	0-2	
1891/92	1	Crewe Alexandra	H	2-2	
	1r	Crewe Alexandra	A	4-1	
	2	Sheffield United	H	3-1	
	QF	Aston Villa	H	1-3	
1892/93	1	Bolton Wanderers	A	1-1	
	1r	Bolton Wanderers	H	2-1	
	2	Middlesbrough	H	2-1	
	QF	Darwen	H	5-0	
	SF	Blackburn Rovers	N	2-1	At Town Ground, Nottingham
	F	Everton	N	1-0	At Fallowfield
1893/94	1	Aston Villa	A	2-4	
1894/95	1	Darwen	A	0-0	
	1r	Darwen	H	2-0	
	2	Stoke	H	2-0	
	QF	West Bromwich Albion	A	0-1	
1895/96	1	Notts County	H	2-2	
	1r	Notts County	A	4-3	
	2	Liverpool	H	2-0	
	QF	Stoke	H	3-0	
	SF	Derby County	N	2-1	At Perry Barr, Birmingham
	F	Sheffield Wednesday	N	1-2	At Crystal Palace
1896/97	1	Millwall Athletic	A	2-1	
	2	Blackburn Rovers	A	1-2	
1897/98	1	Notts County	A	1-0	
	2	Derby County	H	0-1	
1898/99	1	Bolton Wanderers	H	0-0	
	1r	Bolton Wanderers	A	1-0	
	2	Derby County	A	1-2	
1899/1900	1	Queens Park Rangers	A	1-1	

	1r	Queens Park Rangers	H	0-1	
1900/01	1	New Brighton Tower	H	5-1	
	2	Notts County	A	3-2	
	QF	Sheffield United	H	0-4	
1901/02	1	Bolton Wanderers	H	0-2	
1902/03	1	Bury	A	0-1	
1903/04	1	Stockton	A	4-1	
	2	Derby County	A	2-2	
	2r	Derby County	H	2-2	
	2r2	Derby County	N	0-1	At Aston Villa
1904/05	1	Sunderland	A	1-1	
	1r	Sunderland	H	1-0	
	2	Southampton	H	2-3	
1905/06	1	Bishop Auckland	A	3-0	
	2	Bradford City	A	0-5	
1906/07	1	Sheffield Wednesday	A	2-3	
1907/08	1	Bradford City	A	1-1	
	1r	Bradford City	H	1-0	
	2	Bury	H	2-0	
	3	Swindon Town	H	2-0	
	QF	Stoke	A	1-0	
	SF	Southampton	N	2-0	At Chelsea
	F	Newcastle United	N	3-1	At Crystal Palace
1908/09	1	Crystal Palace	H	2-2	
	1r	Crystal Palace	A	2-4	
1909/10	1	Reading	H	5-0	
	2	West Ham United	H	1-5	
1910/11	1	Accrington Stanley	H	2-0	
	2	Manchester City	H	1-0	
	3	Chelsea	H	0-2	
1911/12	1	Watford	A	0-0	
	1r	Watford	H	10-0	
	2	Lincoln City	H	2-1	
	3	Blackburn Rovers	A	2-3	
1912/13	1	London Caledonians	H	3-1	
	2	Bradford Park Avenue	A	0-3	
1913/14	1	Southampton	H	3-0	
	2	Sheffield Wednesday	H	1-1	
	2r	Sheffield Wednesday	A	0-1	
1914/15	1	Reading	A	1-0	
	2	Sheffield Wednesday	A	0-2	
1919/20	1	Blackburn Rovers	A	2-2	
	1r	Blackburn Rovers	H	1-0	
	2	Cardiff City	H	1-2	
1920/21	1	Stoke	H	3-2	
	2	Derby County	A	1-1	
	2r	Derby County	H	1-0	
	3	Fulham	A	1-0	
	QF	Everton	A	1-0	
	SF	Cardiff City	N	0-0	At Liverpool
	SFr	Cardiff City	N	3-1	At Manchester United
	F	Tottenham Hotspur	N	0-1	At Chelsea
1921/22	1	Preston North End	A	0-3	
1922/23	1	Merthyr Town	A	1-0	
	2	Liverpool	H	0-2	

1923/24	1	Darlington	H	3-1	
	2	Charlton Athletic	A	0-0	
	2r	Charlton Athletic	H	1-0	
	3	West Bromwich Albion	A	1-1	
	3r	West Bromwich Albion	H	0-2	
1924/25	1	Hull City	A	1-1	
	1r	Hull City	H	0-1	
1925/26	3	Arsenal	H	1-1	
	3r	Arsenal	A	0-1	
1926/27	3	Carlisle United	A	2-0	
	4	Nottingham Forest	H	2-0	
	5	Hull City	H	1-0	
	QF	Arsenal	A	1-2	
1927/28	3	Chelsea	H	2-1	
	4	Sheffield United	A	1-3	
1928/29	3	Mansfield Town	H	0-1	
1929/30	3	Oldham Athletic	A	0-1	
1930/31	3	Wrexham	H	9-1	
	4	Bradford City	A	0-0	
	4r	Bradford City	H	4-2	
	5	Barnsley	A	3-1	
	QF	West Bromwich Albion	A	1-1	
	QFr	West Bromwich Albion	H	1-2	
1931/32	3	Luton Town	A	2-1	
	4	Preston North End	A	0-2	
1932/33	3	Derby County	H	3-6	
1933/34	3	Newcastle United	H	1-0	
	4	Derby County	A	0-3	
1934/35	3	Notts County	H	4-0	
	4	Sheffield Wednesday	H	1-2	
1935/36	3	Leeds United	H	1-1	
	3r	Leeds United	A	1-3	
1936/37	3	Middlesbrough	H	6-1	
	4	Sheffield United	H	2-2	
	4r	Sheffield United	A	2-1	
	5	Grimsby Town	A	1-1	
	5r	Grimsby Town	H	6-2	
	QF	Sunderland	H	1-1	
	QFr	Sunderland	A	2-2	
	QFr2	Sunderland	N	0-4	At Sheffield Wednesday
1937/38	3	Swansea Town	A	4-0	
	4	Arsenal	H	1-2	
1938/39	3	Bradford Park Avenue	H	3-1	
	4	Leicester City	H	5-1	
	5	Liverpool	H	4-1	
	QF	Everton	H	2-0	
	SF	Grimsby Town	N	5-0	At Manchester United
	F	Portsmouth	N	1-4	At Wembley
1945/46	3(1)	Lovells Athletic	A	4-2	
	3(2)	Lovells Athletic	H	8-1	
	4(1)	Charlton Athletic	A	2-5	
	4(2)	Charlton Athletic	H	1-1	
1946/47	3	Rotherham United	H	3-0	
	4	Sheffield United	H	0-0	
	4r	Sheffield United	A	0-2	

1947/48	3	Bournemouth & Boscombe	A	2-1	
	4	Everton	H	1-1	
	4r	Everton	A	2-3	
1948/49	3	Chesterfield	H	6-0	
	4	Sheffield United	A	3-0	
	5	Liverpool	H	3-1	
	QF	West Bromwich Albion	H	1-0	
	SF	Manchester United	N	1-1	At Sheffield Wednesday
	SFr	Manchester United	N	1-0	At Everton
	F	Leicester City	N	3-1	At Wembley
1949/50	3	Plymouth Argyle	A	1-1	
	3r	Plymouth Argyle	H	3-0	
	4	Sheffield United	H	0-0	
	4r	Sheffield United	A	4-3	
	5	Blackpool	H	0-0	
	5r	Blackpool	A	0-1	
1950/51	3	Plymouth Argyle	A	2-1	
	4	Aston Villa	H	3-1	
	5	Huddersfield Town	H	2-0	
	QF	Sunderland	A	1-1	
	QFr	Sunderland	H	3-1	
	SF	Newcastle United	N	0-0	At Sheffield Wednesday
	SFr	Newcastle United	N	1-2	At Huddersfield Town
1951/52	3	Manchester City	A	2-2	
	3r	Manchester City	H	4-1	
	4	Liverpool	A	1-2	
1952/53	3	Preston North End	A	2-5	
1953/54	3	Birmingham City	H	1-2	
1954/55	3	Grimsby Town	A	5-2	
	4	Arsenal	H	1-0	
	5	Charlton Athletic	H	4-1	
	QF	Sunderland	A	0-2	
1955/56	3	West Bromwich Albion	H	1-2	
1956/57	3	Swansea Town	H	5-3	
	4	Bournemouth & Boscombe	H	0-1	
1957/58	3	Lincoln City	A	1-0	
	4	Portsmouth	H	5-1	
	5	Darlington	H	6-1	
	QF	Bolton Wanderers	A	1-2	
1958/59	3	Barrow	A	4-2	
	4	Bolton Wanderers	H	1-2	
1959/60	3	Newcastle United	A	2-2	
	3r	Newcastle United	H	4-2	
	4	Charlton Athletic	H	2-1	
	5	Luton Town	A	4-1	
	QF	Leicester City	A	2-1	
	SF	Aston Villa	N	1-0	At West Bromwich Albion
	F	Blackburn Rovers	N	3-0	At Wembley
1960/61	3	Huddersfield Town	H	1-1	
	3r	Huddersfield Town	A	1-2	
1961/62	3	Carlisle United	H	3-1	
	4	West Bromwich Albion	H	1-2	
1962/63	3	Nottingham Forest	A	3-4	
1963/64	3	Arsenal	A	1-2	
1964/65	3	Portsmouth	A	0-0	

	3r	Portsmouth	H	3-2	
	4	Rotherham United	H	2-2	
	4r	Rotherham United	A	3-0	
	5	Aston Villa	A	1-1	
	5r	Aston Villa	H	0-0	
	5r2	Aston Villa	N	3-1	At West Bromwich Albion
	QF	Manchester United	H	3-5	
1965/66	3	Altrincham	H	5-0	
	4	Sheffield United	H	3-0	
	5	Manchester United	H	2-4	
1966/67	3	Oldham Athletic	A	2-2	
	3r	Oldham Athletic	H	4-1	
	4	Everton	H	1-1	
	4r	Everton	A	1-3	
1967/68	3	Rotherham United	A	0-1	
1968/69	3	Hull City	A	3-1	
	4	Tottenham Hotspur	A	1-2	
1969/70	3	Burnley	A	0-3	
1970/71	3	Norwich City	H	5-1	
	4	Derby County	A	1-2	
1971/72	3	Leicester City	H	1-1	
	3r	Leicester City	A	0-2	
1972/73	3	Manchester United	H	1-0	
	4	Bristol City	H	1-0	
	5	Millwall	H	1-0	
	QF	Coventry City	H	2-0	
	SF	Leeds United	N	0-1	At Manchester City
1973/74	3	Leeds United	H	1-1	
	3r	Leeds United	A	0-1	
1974/75	3	Ipswich Town	H	1-2	
1975/76	3	Arsenal	H	3-0	
	4	Ipswich Town	A	0-0	
	4r	Ipswich Town	H	1-0	
	5	Charlton Athletic	H	3-0	
	QF	Manchester United	A	1-1	
	QFr	Manchester United	H	2-3	
1976/77	3	Rotherham United	H	3-2	
	4	Ipswich Town	A	2-2	
	4r	Ipswich Town	H	1-0	
	5	Chester	H	1-0	
	QF	Leeds United	H	0-1	
1977/78	3	Exeter City	A	2-2	
	3r	Exeter City	H	3-1	
	4	Arsenal	A	1-2	
1978/79	3	Brighton & Hove Albion	A	3-2	
	4	Newcastle United	A	1-1	
	4r	Newcastle United	H	1-0	
	5	Crystal Palace	A	1-0	
	QF	Shrewsbury Town	H	1-1	
	QFr	Shrewsbury Town	A	3-1	
	SF	Arsenal	N	0-2	At Aston Villa
1979/80	3	Notts County	A	3-0	
	4	Norwich City	H	1-1	
	4r	Norwich City	A	3-2	

	5	Watford	H	0-3	
1980/81	3	Stoke City	A	2-2	
	3r	Stoke City	H	2-1	
	4	Watford	A	1-1	
	4r	Watford	H	2-1	
	5	Wrexham	H	3-1	
	QF	Middlesbrough	A	1-1	
	QFr	Middlesbrough	H	3-1	
	SF	Tottenham Hotspur	N	2-2	At Sheffield Wednesday
	SFr	Tottenham Hotspur	N	0-3	At Arsenal
1981/82	3	Leeds United	H	1-3	
1982/83	3	Tranmere Rovers	A	1-0	
	4	Aston Villa	A	0-1	
1983/84	3	Coventry City	A	1-1	
	3r	Coventry City	H	1-1	
	3r2	Coventry City	A	0-3	
1984/85	3	Huddersfield Town	H	1-1	
	3r	Huddersfield Town	A	1-3	
1985/86	1	Rotherham United	A	0-6	
1986/87	1	Chorley	A	1-1	At Bolton Wanderers
	1r	Chorley	H	1-1	
	1r2	Chorley	A	0-3	At Bolton Wanderers
1987/88	1	Cheltenham Town	H	5-1	
	2	Wigan Athletic	A	3-1	
	3	Bradford City	A	1-2	
1988/89	1	Grimsby Town	A	0-1	
1989/90	3	Sheffield Wednesday	H	1-2	
1990/91	3	Cambridge United	H	0-1	
1991/92	3	Nottingham Forest	A	0-1	
1992/93	3	Watford	A	4-1	
	4	Bolton Wanderers	H	0-2	
1993/94	3	Crystal Palace	H	1-0	
	4	Port Vale	A	2-0	
	5	Ipswich Town	H	1-1	
	5r	Ipswich Town	A	2-1	
	QF	Chelsea	A	0-1	
1994/95	3	Mansfield Town	A	3-2	
	4	Sheffield Wednesday	A	0-0	
	4r	Sheffield Wednesday	H	1-1	Wolves won 4-3 on penalties
	5	Leicester City	H	1-0	
	QF	Crystal Palace	A	1-1	
	QFr	Crystal Palace	H	1-4	
1995/96	3	Birmingham City	A	1-1	
	3r	Birmingham City	H	2-1	
	4	Tottenham Hotspur	A	1-1	
	4r	Tottenham Hotspur	H	0-2	
1996/97	3	Portsmouth	H	1-2	
1997/98	3	Darlington	A	4-0	
	4	Charlton Athletic	A	1-1	
	4r	Charlton Athletic	H	3-0	
	5	Wimbledon	A	1-1	
	5r	Wimbledon	H	2-1	
	QF	Leeds United	A	1-0	
	SF	Arsenal	N	0-1	At Aston Villa

1998/99	3	Bolton Wanderers	A	2-1	
	4	Arsenal	H	1-2	
1999/2000	3	Wigan Athletic	A	1-0	
	4	Sheffield Wednesday	A	1-1	
	4r	Sheffield Wednesday	H	0-0	Sheffield Wednesday won 4-3 on penalties
2000/01	3	Nottingham Forest	A	1-0	
	4	Wycombe Wanderers	A	1-2	
2001/02	3	Gillingham	H	0-1	
2002/03	3	Newcastle United	H	3-2	
	4	Leicester City	H	4-1	
	5	Rochdale	H	3-1	
	QF	Southampton	A	0-2	
2003/04	3	Kidderminster Harriers	A	1-1	
	3r	Kidderminster Harriers	H	2-0	
	4	West Ham United	H	1-3	
2004/05	3	Millwall	H	2-0	
	4	Arsenal	A	0-2	
2005/06	3	Plymouth Argyle	H	1-0	
	4	Manchester United	H	0-3	
2006/07	3	Oldham Athletic	H	2-2	
	3r	Oldham Athletic	A	2-0	
	4	West Bromwich Albion	H	0-3	
2007/08	3	Cambridge United	H	2-1	
	4	Watford	A	4-1	
	5	Cardiff City	A	0-2	
2008/09	3	Birmingham City	A	2-0	
	4	Middlesbrough	H	1-2	
2009/10	3	Tranmere Rovers	A	1-0	
	4	Crystal Palace	H	2-2	
	4r	Crystal Palace	A	1-3	
2010/11	3	Doncaster Rovers	A	2-2	
	3r	Doncaster Rovers	H	5-0	
	4	Stoke City	H	0-1	
2011/12	3	Birmingham City	A	0-0	
	3r	Birmingham City	H	0-1	
2012/13	3	Luton Town	A	0-1	
2013/14	1	Oldham Athletic	A	1-1	
	1r	Oldham Athletic	H	1-2	
2014/15	3	Fulham	A	0-0	
	3r	Fulham	H	3-3	Fulham won 5-3 on penalties

(Courtesy of F. C. H. D. – The Football Club History Database)

FOOTBALL LEAGUE CUP: COMPLETE HISTORY

SEASON	RD	OPPONENTS	VEN	SCORE
1966/67	2	Mansfield Town	H	2-1
	3	Fulham	A	0-5
1967/68	2	Huddersfield Town	A	0-1
1968/69	2	Southend United	H	1-0

	3	Millwall	H	5-1	
	4	Blackpool	A	1-2	
1969/70	2	Tottenham Hotspur	H	1-0	
	3	Brighton & Hove Albion	A	3-2	
	4	Queens Park Rangers	A	1-3	
1970/71	2	Oxford United	A	0-1	
1971/72	2	Manchester City	A	3-4	
1972/73	2	Orient	H	2-1	
	3	Sheffield Wednesday	H	3-1	
	4	Bristol Rovers	H	4-0	
	QF	Blackpool	H	1-1	
	QFr	Blackpool	A	1-0	
	SF(1)	Tottenham Hotspur	H	1-2	
	SF(2)	Tottenham Hotspur	A	2-2	Tottenham won 4-3 on aggregate
1973/74	2	Halifax Town	A	3-0	
	3	Tranmere Rovers	A	1-1	
	3r	Tranmere Rovers	H	2-1	
	4	Exeter City	H	5-1	
	QF	Liverpool	H	1-0	
	SF(1)	Norwich City	A	1-1	
	SF(2)	Norwich City	H	1-0	Wolves won 2-1 on aggregate
	F	Manchester City	N	2-1	At Wembley
1974/75	2	Fulham	H	1-3	
1975/76	2	Swindon Town	A	2-2	
	2r	Swindon Town	H	3-2	
	3	Birmingham City	A	2-0	
	4	Mansfield Town	A	0-1	
1976/77	2	Sheffield Wednesday	H	1-2	
1977/78	2	Luton Town	H	1-3	
1978/79	2	Reading	A	0-1	
1979/80	2(1)	Burnley	A	1-1	
	2(2)	Burnley	H	2-0	Wolves won 3-1 on aggregate
	3	Crystal Palace	A	2-1	
	4	Queens Park Rangers	A	1-1	
	4r	Queens Park Rangers	H	1-0	
	QF	Grimsby Town	A	0-0	
	QFr	Grimsby Town	H	1-1	
	QFr2	Grimsby Town	N	2-0	At Derby County
	SF(1)	Swindon Town	A	1-2	
	SF(2)	Swindon Town	H	3-1	Wolves won 4-3 on aggregate
	F	Nottingham Forest	N	1-0	At Wembley
1980/81	2(1)	Cambridge United	A	1-3	
	2(2)	Cambridge United	H	0-1	Cambridge Utd won 4-1 on aggregate
1981/82	2(1)	Aston Villa	A	2-3	
	2(2)	Aston Villa	H	1-2	Aston Villa won 5-3 on aggregate
1982/83	2(1)	Sunderland	H	1-1	
	2(2)	Sunderland	A	0-5	Sunderland won 6-1 on aggregate
1983/84	2(1)	Preston North End	H	2-3	
	2(2)	Preston North End	A	0-1	Preston North End won 4-2 on aggregate
1984/85	2(1)	Port Vale	A	2-1	
	2(2)	Port Vale	H	0-0	Wolves won 2-1 on aggregate
	3	Southampton	A	2-2	
	3r	Southampton	H	0-2	
1985/86	1(1)	Walsall	A	1-1	
	1(2)	Walsall	H	0-1	Walsall won 2-1 on aggregate
1986/87	1(1)	Lincoln City	H	1-2	

	1(2)	Lincoln City	A	1-0	Aggregate 2-2, Lincoln City won on away goals
1987/88	1(1)	Notts County	H	3-0	
	1(2)	Notts County	A	2-1	Wolves won 5-1 on aggregate
	2(1)	Manchester City	A	2-1	
	2(2)	Manchester City	H	0-2	Man City won 3-2 on aggregate
1988/89	1(1)	Birmingham City	H	3-2	
	1(2)	Birmingham City	A	0-1	Aggregate 3-3, Birmingham City won on away goals
1989/90	1(1)	Lincoln City	H	1-0	
	1(2)	Lincoln City	A	2-0	Wolves won 3-0 on aggregate
	2(1)	Aston Villa	A	1-2	
	2(2)	Aston Villa	H	1-1	Aston Villa won 3-2 on aggregate
1990/91	2(1)	Hull City	A	0-0	
	2(2)	Hull City	H	1-1	Aggregate 1-1, Hull City won on away goals
1991/92	2(1)	Shrewsbury Town	H	6-1	
	2(2)	Shrewsbury Town	A	1-3	Wolves won 7-4 on aggregate
	3	Everton	A	1-4	
1992/93	2(1)	Notts County	A	2-3	
	2(2)	Notts County	H	0-1	Notts County won 4-2 on aggregate
1993/94	2(1)	Swindon Town	A	0-2	
	2(2)	Swindon Town	H	2-1	Swindon Town won 3-2 on aggregate
1994/95	2(1)	Chesterfield	A	3-1	
	2(2)	Chesterfield	H	1-1	Wolves won 4-2 on aggregate
	3	Nottingham Forest	H	2-3	
1995/96	2(1)	Fulham	H	2-0	
	2(2)	Fulham	A	5-1	Wolves won 7-1 on aggregate
	3	Charlton Athletic	H	0-0	
	3r	Charlton Athletic	A	2-1	
	4	Coventry City	H	2-1	
	QF	Aston Villa	A	0-1	
1996/97	1(1)	Swindon Town	A	0-2	
	1(2)	Swindon Town	H	1-0	Swindon Town won 2-1 on aggregate
1997/98	1(1)	Queens Park Rangers	A	2-0	
	1(2)	Queens Park Rangers	H	1-2	Wolves won 3-2 on aggregate
	2(1)	Fulham	A	1-0	
	2(2)	Fulham	H	1-0	Wolves won 2-0 on aggregate
	3	Reading	A	2-4	
1998/99	1(1)	Barnet	A	1-2	
	1(2)	Barnet	H	5-0	Wolves won 6-2 on aggregate
	2(1)	AFC Bournemouth	A	1-1	
	2(2)	AFC Bournemouth	H	1-2	AFC Bournemouth won 3-2 on aggregate
1999/2000	1(1)	Wycombe Wanderers	A	1-0	
	1(2)	Wycombe Wanderers	H	2-4	Wycombe won 4-3 on aggregate
2000/01	1(1)	Oxford United	H	0-1	
	1(2)	Oxford United	A	3-1	Wolves won 3-2 on aggregate
	2(1)	Grimsby Town	A	2-3	
	2(2)	Grimsby Town	H	2-0	Wolves won 4-3 on aggregate
	3	Fulham	A	2-3	
2001/02	1	Swindon Town	H	1-2	
2002/03	1	Swansea City	A	3-2	
	2	Rotherham United	A	4-4	Rotherham United won 4-2 on penalties
2003/04	2	Darlington	H	2-0	
	3	Burnley	H	2-0	
	4	Arsenal	A	1-5	
2004/05	1	Rochdale	A	4-2	
	2	Burnley	A	1-1	Burnley won 4-2 on penalties
2005/06	1	Chester City	H	5-1	

	2	Watford	A	1-2	
2006/07	1	Chesterfield	A	0-0	Chesterfield won 6-5 on penalties
2007/08	1	Bradford City	H	2-1	
	2	Morecambe	H	1-3	
2008/09	1	Accrington Stanley	H	3-2	
	2	Rotherham United	A	0-0	Rotherham United won 4-3 on penalties
2009/10	2	Swindon Town	H	0-0	Wolves won 6-5 on penalties
	3	Manchester United	A	0-1	
2010/11	2	Southend United	H	2-1	
	3	Notts County	H	4-2	
	4	Manchester United	A	2-3	
2011/12	2	Northampton Town	A	4-0	
	3	Millwall	H	5-0	
	4	Manchester City	H	2-5	
2012/13	1	Aldershot Town	H	1-1	Wolves won 7-6 on penalties
	2	Northampton Town	A	2-1	
	3	Chelsea	A	0-6	
2013/14	1	Morecambe	A	0-1	
2014/15	1	Northampton Town	H	2-3	

(Courtesy of F. C. H. D. – The Football Club History Database)

THE BLACK COUNTRY DERBY: COMPLETE RECORD

WBA *v.* Wolves

Season	League	Results
2011/12	Premier League	WBA 2-0 Wolves (24,872)
		Wolves 1-5 WBA (27,131)
2010/11	Premier League	Wolves 3-1 WBA (28,510)
		WBA 1-1 Wolves (26,170)
2007/08	Championship	Wolves 0-1 WBA (27,883)
		WBA 0-0 Wolves (27,493)
2006/07	Championship Play-off	WBA 1-0 Wolves (27,415)
		Wolves 2-3 WBA (27,750)
	FA Cup Round 4	Wolves 0-3 WBA (28,107)
	Championship	Wolves 1-0 WBA (28,016)
		WBA 3-0 Wolves (26,606)
2001/02	Division One	Wolves 0-1 WBA (27,515)
		WBA 1-1 Wolves (26,143)
2000/01	Division One	Wolves 3-1 WBA (25,069)
		WBA 1-0 Wolves (21,492)
1999/2000	Division One	WBA 1-1 Wolves (21,097)
		Wolves 1-1 WBA (25,500)

1998/99	Division One	Wolves 1-1 WBA (27,038)
		WBA 2-0 Wolves (22,682)
1997/98	Division One	Wolves 0-1 WBA (28,244)
		WBA 1-0 Wolves (22,511)
1996/97	Division One	Wolves 2-0 WBA (27,336)
		WBA 2-4 Wolves (21,791)
1995/96	Division One	WBA 1-1 Wolves (21,658)
		Wolves 1-1 WBA (26,329)
1994/95	Division One	WBA 2-0 Wolves (20,661)
		Wolves 2-0 WBA (27,764)
1993/94	Division One	Wolves 1-2 WBA (28,039)
		WBA 3-2 Wolves (26,615)
1990/91	Division One	Wolves 2-2 WBA (22,982)
		WBA 1-1 Wolves (28,310)
1989/90	Division One	Wolves 2-1 WBA (24,475)
		WBA 1-2 Wolves (21,316)
1983/84	Division One	Wolves 0-0 WBA (13,208)
		WBA 1-3 Wolves (18,914)
1981/82	Division One	Wolves 1-2 WBA (19,813)
		WBA 3-0 Wolves (23,329)
1980/81	Division One	Wolves 2-0 WBA (29,764)
		WBA 1-1 Wolves (26,324)
1979/80	Division One	WBA 0-0 Wolves (30,843)
		Wolves 0-0 WBA (32,564)
1978/79	Division One	WBA 1-1 Wolves (32,395)
		Wolves 0-3 WBA (29,117)
1977/78	Division One	Wolves 1-1 WBA (29,757)
		WBA 2-2 Wolves (31,359)
1972/73	Division One	Wolves 2-0 WBA (33,520)
		WBA 1-0 Wolves (31,121)
1971/72	Division One	Wolves 0-1 WBA (30,319)
		WBA 2-3 Wolves (37,696)
1970/71	Division One	WBA 2-4 Wolves (36,754)
		Wolves 2-1 WBA (39,300)
1969/70	Division One	WBA 3-3 Wolves (37,819)
		Wolves 1-0 WBA (39,832)
1968/69	Division One	Wolves 0-1 WBA (37,920)
		WBA 0-0 Wolves (40,175)
1967/68	Division One	WBA 4-1 Wolves (44,573)
		Wolves 3-3 WBA (52,438)

1964/65	Division One	Wolves 3-2 WBA (26,722)
		WBA 5-1 Wolves (23,006)
1963/64	Division One	WBA 3-1 -Wolves (19,839)
		Wolves 0-0 WBA (37,338)
1962/63	Division One	WBA 2-2 Wolves (15,517)
		Wolves 7-0 WBA (22,618)
1961/62	FA Cup Round 4	Wolves 1-2 WBA (46,411)
	Division One	Wolves 1-5 WBA (20,558)
		WBA 1-1 Wolves (24,778)
1960/61	Division One	WBA 2-1 Wolves (34,108)
		Wolves 4-2 WBA (31,385)
1959/60	Division One	Wolves 3-1 WBA (49,791)
		WBA 0-1 Wolves (48,739)
1958/59	Division One	Wolves 5-2 WBA (44,240)
		WBA 2-1 Wolves (55,498)
1957/58	Division One	WBA 0-3 Wolves (56,904)
		Wolves 1-1 WBA (55,618)
1956/57	Division One	Wolves 5-2 WBA (27,942)
		WBA 1-1 Wolves (34,379)
1955/56	FA Cup Round 3	Wolves 1-2 WBA (55,564)
	Division One	Wolves 3-2 WBA (31,068)
		WBA 1-1 Wolves (50,306)
1954/55	Charity Shield	Wolves 4-4 WBA (45,035)
	Division One	WBA 1-0 Wolves (28,573)
		Wolves 4-0 WBA (55,374)
1953/54	Division One	WBA 0-1 Wolves (58,884)
		Wolves 1-0 WBA (56,590)
1952/53	Division One	Wolves 2-0 WBA (48,375)
		WBA 1-1 Wolves (54,480)
1951/52	Division One	Wolves 1-4 WBA (48,940)
		WBA 2-1 Wolves (36,429)
1950/51	Division One	WBA 3-2 Wolves (39,066)
		Wolves 3-1 WBA (45,087)
1949/50	Division One	WBA 1-1 Wolves (60,945)
		Wolves 1-1 WBA (56,661)
1948/49	FA Cup Round 6	Wolves 1-0 WBA (55,684)
1937/38	Division One	Wolves 2–1 WBA (43,639)
		WBA 2–2 Wolves (55,444)
1936/37	Division One	Wolves 5-2 WBA (28,486)
		WBA 2-1 Wolves (33,962)

1935/36	Division One	Wolves 2-0 WBA (34,790)
		WBA 2-1 Wolves (43,406)
1934/35	Division One	WBA 5-2 Wolves (31,494)
		Wolves 3-2 WBA (35,386)
1933/34	Division One	WBA 2-0 Wolves (24,892)
		Wolves 0-0 WBA (37,308)
1932/33	Division One	Wolves 3-3 WBA (34,534)
		WBA 4-1 Wolves (31,068)
1930/31	FA Cup Round 6	WBA 1-1 Wolves (52,385)
	FA Cup Round 6 Replay	Wolves 1-2 WBA (46,860)
	Division Two	Wolves 1-4 WBA (36,054)
		WBA 2-1 Wolves (40,065)
1929/30	Division Two	WBA 7-3 Wolves (20,311)
		Wolves 2-4 WBA (25,961)
1928/29	Division Two	Wolves 0-1 WBA (24,340)
		WBA 0-2 Wolves (24,902)
1927/28	Division Two	WBA 4-0 Wolves (37,342)
		Wolves 4-1 WBA (40,816)
1923/24	FA Cup Round 3	WBA 1-1 Wolves (55,849)
	FA Cup Round 3 Replay	Wolves 0-2 WBA (40,083)
1910/11	Division Two	WBA 2-1 Wolves (26,303)
		Wolves 2-3 WBA (18,500)
1909/10	Division Two	WBA 0-1 Wolves (24,899)
		Wolves 3-1 WBA (24,000)
1908/09	Division Two	Wolves 0-1 WBA (20,000)
		WBA 0-2 Wolves (30,600)
1907/08	Division Two	WBA 1-0 Wolves (30,026)
		Wolves 1-2 WBA (24,000)
1906/07	Division Two	WBA 1-1 Wolves (28,000)
		Wolves 0-3 WBA (25,000)
1903/04	Division One	WBA 1-2 Wolves (6,338)
		Wolves 1-0 WBA (12,431)
1902/03	Division One	WBA 2-2 Wolves (26,081)
		Wolves 1-2 WBA (14,072)
1900/01	Division One	WBA 1-2 Wolves (18,188)
		Wolves 0-0 WBA (12,000)
1899/1900	Division One	WBA 3-2 Wolves (6,680)
		Wolves 2-0 WBA (10,089)
1898/99	Division One	Wolves 5-1 WBA (12,052)
		WBA 1-2 Wolves (6,457)

1897/98	Division One	Wolves 1-1 WBA (8,100)
		WBA 2-2 Wolves (11,750)
1896/97	Division One	Wolves 6-1 WBA (11,561)
		WBA 1-0 Wolves (6,000)
1895/96	Division One	Wolves 1-2 WBA (8,114)
		WBA 2-1 Wolves (3,000)
1894/95	FA Cup Round 3	WBA 1-0 Wolves (20,977)
	Division One	Wolves 3-1 WBA (6,500)
		WBA 5-1 Wolves (5,100)
1893/94	Division One	Wolves 0-8 WBA (8,000)
		WBA 0-0 Wolves (10,000)
1892/93	Division One	Wolves 1-1 WBA (8,000)
		WBA 2–1 Wolves (4,000)
1891/92	Division One	Wolves 2-1 WBA (7,200)
		WBA 4-3 Wolves (10,000)
1890/91	Division One	Wolves 4-0 WBA (9,300)
		WBA 0-1 Wolves (4,300)
1889/90	Division One	Wolves 1-1 WBA (8,500)
		WBA 1-4 Wolves (5,550)
1888/89	Division One	WBA 1-3 Wolves (4,000)
		Wolves 2-1 WBA (8,600)
1887/88	FA Cup Round 3	WBA 2-0 Wolves (7,429)
1885/86	FA Cup Round 4	WBA 3-1 Wolves (5,196)

Statistics

	West Brom Wins	Draws	Wolves wins
League	54	40	52
Play-offs	2	0	0
FA Cup	8	2	1
Charity Shield	0	1	0
Total	64	43	53

(*Source: Wikipedia*)

AND FINALLY

We couldn't end this book without playing tribute to the greatest
Wolverhampton Wanderers player of all time – Steve Bull. Brief facts
are below as well as the date, opposition and competition of every
goal he scored for the club…

Club legend: Steve Bull
Born: 28 March 1966 in Tipton
Height: 5 foot 11 inches
Playing Position: Striker
Previous Club: West Bromwich Albion (9 games, 3 goals)
Wolves Record: 561 appearances, 306 goals (18 hat-tricks)
Debut: 22 November 1986 *v.* Wrexham
First goal for Wolves: 2 December 1986 v. Cardiff (Freight Rover Trophy)
International: Bull scored four goals for England from 13 appearances

Bully's Complete Goals Record – Who He Scored Them Against, How Many and When

Goal No.	Date	Opposition	H/A	Score	Competition
Season 1986/87					
1	12/2/1986	Cardiff City	Away	1-0	FRT
2	12/13/1986	Hartlepool	Away	1-0	Div 4
3/4	12/16/1986	Bournemouth	Home	4-3	FRT
5	12/20/1986	Southend Utd	Home	1-2	Div 4
6	12/27/1986	Exeter City	Home	2-2	Div 4
7	1/24/1987	Cardiff City	Away	2-0	Div 4
8	2/7/1987	Stockport Co.	Home	3-1	Div 4
9	3/3/1987	Colchester Utd	Home	2-0	Div 4
10	3/7/1987	Leyton Orient	Away	1-3	Div 4
11	3/28/1987	Scunthorpe Utd	Away	1-0	Div 4
12	4/18/1987	Peterborough	Home	1-0	Div 4
13/14	5/2/1987	Lincoln City	Home	3-0	Div 4
15	5/4/1987	Exeter City	Away	3-1	Div 4
16/17/18	5/9/1987	Hartlepool	Home	4-1	Div 4
19	5/17/1987	Colchester	Away	2-0	Play-off S/F
Season 1987/88					
20	8/15/1987	Scarborough	Away	2-2	Div 4
21/22	8/25/1987	Notts County	Away	2-1	League Cup
23	8/29/1987	Hereford Utd	Away	2-1	Div 4
24/25	8/31/1987	Scunthorpe	Home	4-1	Div 4
26	9/5/1987	Cardiff City	Away	2-3	Div 4
27	9/12/1987	Crewe Alex	Home	2-2	Div 4
28	9/16/1987	Peterborough	Away	1-1	Div 4
29	9/22/1987	Man City	Away	2-1	League Cup
30	9/26/1987	Torquay	Home	1-2	Div 4
31	9/29/1987	Rochdale	Home	2-0	Div 4
32	10/10/1987	Carlisle	Away	1-0	Div 4

33	10/17/1987	Tranmere	Home	3-0	Div 4
34	10/20/1987	Cambridge	Home	3-0	Div 4
35	10/27/1987	Swansea	Away	1-1	FRT
36	11/3/1987	Swansea	Away	2-1	Div 4
37/38/39	11/14/1987	Cheltenham	Home	5-1	FA Cup
40/41	11/24/1987	Bristol City	Home	3-1	FRT
42/43	12/19/1987	Leyton Orient	Home	2-0	Div 4
44/45	1/1/1988	Hereford	Home	2-0	Div 4
46/47/48	1/19/1988	Brentford	Home	4-0	SVT
49	2/6/1988	Cardiff	Home	1-4	Div 4
50/51	2/9/1988	Peterborough	Home	4-0	SVT
52/53/54	2/13/1988	Exeter	Away	4-2	Div 4
55/56	2/27/1988	Bolton	Home	4-0	Div 4
57	3/8/1988	Torquay	Home	1-0	SVT
58/59/60	3/26/1988	Darlington	Home	5-3	Div 4
61	4/2/1988	Burnley	Away	3-0	Div 4
62/63	4/4/1988	Colchester	Home	2-0	Div 4
64	4/12/1988	Notts County	Away	1-1	SVT
65/66	4/19/1988	Notts County	Home	3-0	SVT
67	4/23/1988	Swansea	Home	2-0	Div 4
68/69	4/26/1988	Newport	Away	3-1	Div 4
70/71	5/2/1988	Hartlepool	Home	2-0	Div 4

Season 1988/89

72/73	8/30/1988	Birmingham	Home	3-2	League Cup
74	9/20/1988	Aldershot	Home	1-0	Div 3
75/76	9/24/1988	Swansea	Away	5-2	Div 3
77/78	10/1/1988	Port Vale	Home	3-3	Div 3
79	10/15/1988	Wigan	Home	2-1	Div 3
80	10/22/1988	Bolton	Away	2-1	Div 3
81	10/29/1988	Gillingham	Away	3-1	Div 3
82	11/5/1988	Southend	Home	3-0	Div 3
83/84	11/12/1988	Huddersfield	Home	4-1	Div 3
85/86/87/88	11/26/1988	Preston	Home	6-0	Div 3
89	11/30/1988	Hereford	Away	2-2	SVT
90/91/92/93	12/13/1988	Port Vale	Home	5-1	SVT
94/95/96	12/17/1988	Mansfield	Home	6-2	Div 3
97	12/31/1988	Brentford	Away	2-2	Div 3
98	1/2/1989	Chester	Home	3-1	Div 3
99	1/10/1989	Cardiff	Home	2-0	Div 3
100/101/102	1/24/1989	Bristol City	Home	3-0	SVT
103/104/105	2/11/1989	Fulham	Home	5-2	Div 3
106	2/28/1989	Blackpool	Away	2-0	Div 3
107	3/4/1989	Bolton	Home	1-0	Div 3
108	3/14/1989	Gillingham	Home	6-1	Div 3
109/110/111	3/18/1989	Bury	Home	4-0	Div 3
112	3/22/1989	Hereford	Away	2-0	SVT
113	4/1/1989	Mansfield	Away	1-3	Div 3
114	4/8/1989	Brentford	Home	2-0	Div 3
115/116	4/12/1989	Torquay	Away	2-1	SVT
117	4/15/1989	Aldershot	Away	2-1	Div 3
118/119	5/1/1989	Bristol City	Home	2-0	Div 3
120	5/6/1989	Northampton	Home	3-2	Div 3
121	5/9/1989	Sheffield Utd	Home	2-2	Div 3

Season 1989/90

122	8/26/1989	Bradford	Home	1-1	Div 2
123	8/30/1989	Lincoln	Away	2-0	League Cup
124	9/12/1989	Brighton	Home	2-4	Div 2
125/126	9/26/1989	Barnsley	Away	2-2	Div 2
127/128	9/30/1989	Portsmouth	Home	5-0	Div 2
129	10/4/1989	A Villa	Home	1-1	League Cup
130	10/15/1989	WBA	Away	2-1	Div 2
131	10/17/1989	Port Vale	Home	2-0	Div 2
132	11/4/1989	West Ham	Home	1-0	Div 2
133	12/26/1989	Hull	Home	1-2	Div 2
134/135/136/137	1/1/1990	Newcastle	Away	4-1	Div 2
138	1/6/1990	Sheffield Wed	Home	1-2	FA Cup
139	1/13/1990	Bradford	Away	1-1	Div 2
140	2/10/1990	Ipswich	Home	2-1	Div 2
141	2/24/1990	Watford	Home	1-1	Div 2
142	3/6/1990	Portsmouth	Away	3-1	Div 2
143	3/10/1990	Barnsley	Home	1-1	Div 2
144	3/20/1990	WBA	Home	2-1	Div 2
145/146/147	4/10/1990	Leicester	Home	5-0	Div 2
148	4/21/1990	Oxford	Home	2-0	Div 2

Season 1990/91

149/150	8/25/1990	Oldham	Home	2-3	Div 2
151	8/28/1990	Port Vale	Away	2-1	Div 2
152	9/15/1990	West Ham	Away	1-1	Div 2
153/154	9/22/1990	Plymouth	Home	3-1	Div 2
155/156	10/2/1990	Charlton	Home	3-0	Div 2
157/158/159	10/6/1990	Bristol City	Home	4-0	Div 2
160	10/20/1990	Hull	Away	2-0	Div 2
161	10/23/1990	Middlesbrough	Home	1-0	Div 2
162	11/27/1990	Leicester	Away	1-0	ZDSC
163/164	12/1/1990	Ipswich	Home	2-2	Div 2
165	12/22/1990	Millwall	Home	4-1	Div 2
166	12/26/1990	Sheffield Wed	Away	2-2	Div 2
167	1/12/1991	Brighton	Home	2-3	Div 2
168	2/2/1991	West Ham	Home	2-1	Div 2
169/170	2/26/1991	Port Vale	Home	3-1	Div 2
171	3/5/1991	Leicester	Home	2-1	Div 2
172/173/174	3/16/1991	Oxford	Home	3-3	Div 2
175	3/30/1991	Sheffield Wed	Home	3-2	Div 2

Season 1991/92

176	8/17/1991	Watford	Away	2-0	Div 2
177	8/24/1991	Charlton	Home	1-1	Div 2
178	8/31/1991	Brighton	Away	3-3	Div 2
179	9/7/1991	Oxford	Home	3-1	Div 2
180	9/14/1991	Newcastle	Away	2-1	Div 2
181	9/17/1991	Cambridge	Away	1-2	Div 2
182	9/21/1991	Swindon	Home	2-1	Div 2
183/184	9/24/1991	Shrewsbury	Home	6-1	League Cup
185	10/30/1991	Everton	Away	1-4	League Cup
186/187	11/5/1991	Bristol Rovers	Home	2-3	Div 2
188	12/21/1991	Port Vale	Away	1-1	Div 2
189	1/15/1992	Charlton	Away	2-0	Div 2

190	1/18/1992	Watford	Home	3-0	Div 2
191	2/1/1992	Leicester	Home	1-0	Div 2
192	2/8/1992	Tranmere	Away	3-4	Div 2
193	3/7/1992	Bristol City	Home	1-1	Div 2
194	3/11/1992	Bristol Rovers	Away	1-1	Div 2
195	3/21/1992	Derby	Away	2-1	Div 2
196	3/31/1992	Newcastle	Home	6-2	Div 2
197	4/14/1992	Blackburn	Away	2-1	Div 2
198	4/20/1992	Southend	Home	3-1	Div 2
Season 1992/93					
199	8/15/1992	Brentford	Away	2-0	Div 1
200	8/18/1992	Leicester	Home	3-0	Div 1
201	9/5/1992	Peterborough	Home	4-3	Div 1
202/203	9/19/1992	Watford	Home	2-2	Div 1
204	9/22/1992	Notts County	Away	2-3	League Cup
205	9/30/1992	Peterborough	Home	2-0	AIC
206/207	11/7/1992	Bristol Rovers	Home	5-1	Div 1
208	11/14/1992	Notts County	Away	2-2	Div 1
209	12/5/1992	Cambridge	Away	1-1	Div 1
210	1/2/1993	Watford	Away	4-1	FA Cup
211	2/27/1993	Southend	Home	1-1	Div 1
212	3/6/1993	West Ham	Away	1-3	Div 1
213/214	3/9/1993	Notts County	Home	3-0	Div 1
215	3/13/1993	Bristol Rovers	Away	1-1	Div 1
216	3/20/1993	Cambridge	Home	1-2	Div 1
217	4/7/1993	Luton	Away	1-1	Div 1
Season 1993/94					
218/219	8/14/1993	Bristol City	Home	3-1	Div 1
220	8/25/1993	Millwall	Home	2-0	Div 1
221	8/31/1993	Stoke	Home	3-3	AIC
222	9/5/1993	WBA	Away	2-3	Div 1
223	11/2/1993	Notts County	Home	3-0	Div 1
224/225/226	11/7/1993	Derby	Away	4-0	Div 1
227/228	11/27/1993	Leicester	Away	2-2	Div 1
229	12/5/1993	Derby	Home	2-2	Div 1
230	12/12/1993	Watford	Home	2-0	Div 1
231	12/27/1993	Tranmere	Away	1-1	Div 1
232	5/3/1994	Sunderland	Home	1-1	Div 1
Season 1994/95					
233	9/13/1994	Southend	Home	5-0	Div 1
234	9/17/1994	Burnley	Away	1-0	Div 1
235/236	9/20/1994	Chesterfield	Away	3-1	League Cup
237/238	10/22/1994	Millwall	Home	3-3	Div 1
239	10/30/1994	Stoke	Away	1-1	Div 1
240	12/10/1994	Notts County	Home	1-0	Div 1
241	12/18/1994	Reading	Away	4-2	Div 1
242	12/28/1994	Charlton	Home	2-0	Div 1
243	2/25/1995	Port Vale	Away	4-2	Div 1
244	3/5/1995	Portsmouth	Home	1-0	Div 1
245	3/24/1995	Burnley	Home	2-0	Div 1
246	4/1/1995	Southend	Away	1-0	Div 1
247/248	4/15/1995	Charlton	Away	2-3	Div 1
249	4/22/1995	Sheffield Utd	Away	3-3	Div 1

250	5/3/1995	Tranmere	Away	1-1	Div 1
251	5/14/1995	Bolton	Home	2-1	Play-off S/F

Season 1995/96

252	8/12/1995	Tranmere	Away	2-2	Div 1
253/254	9/9/1995	Grimsby	Home	4-1	Div 1
255	10/28/1995	Sheffield Utd	Home	1-0	Div 1
256	11/25/1995	Huddersfield	Away	1-2	Div 1
257	12/10/1995	Luton	Away	3-2	Div 1
258	12/26/1995	Millwall	Home	1-1	Div 1
259	12/30/1995	Portsmouth	Home	2-2	Div 1
260	1/6/1996	Birmingham	Away	1-1	FA Cup
261	1/17/1996	Birmingham	Home	2-1	FA Cup
262	1/20/1996	Tranmere	Home	2-1	Div 1
263/264	2/17/1996	Norwich	Away	3-2	Div 1
265	2/21/1996	Leicester	Home	2-3	Div 1
266	3/2/1996	Millwall	Away	1-0	Div 1
267	3/23/1996	Birmingham	Home	3-2	Div 1
268	4/8/1996	Barnsley	Home	2-2	Div 1

Season 1996/97

269/270/271	8/17/1996	Grimsby	Away	3-1	Div 1
272	8/24/1996	Bradford	Home	1-0	Div 1
273	9/15/1996	WBA	Away	4-2	Div 1
274	10/13/1996	Southend Utd	Away	1-1	Div 1
275/276	10/13/1996	Portsmouth	Home	2-0	Div 1
277	10/27/1996	Man City	Away	1-0	Div 1
278	11/2/1996	Barnsley	Home	3-3	Div 1
279	11/17/1996	Birmingham	Home	1-2	Div 1
280	12/21/1996	Tranmere	Away	2-0	Div 1
281	1/24/1997	Sheffield Utd	Away	3-2	Div 1
282	1/29/1997	Swindon	Home	1-0	Div 1
283/284	2/1/1997	Stoke	Home	2-0	Div 1
285	2/8/1997	Huddersfield	Away	2-0	Div 1
286	2/22/1997	Barnsley	Away	3-1	Div 1
287	3/4/1997	Birmingham	Away	2-1	Div 1
288/289	3/8/1997	Tranmere	Home	3-2	Div 1
290	3/15/1997	Oldham	Away	2-3	Div 1
291	4/19/1997	Southend Utd	Home	4-1	Div 1

Season 1997/98

292/293	8/30/1997	Bury	Home	4-2	Div 1
294	9/3/1997	Port Vale	Home	1-1	Div 1
295/296	9/13/1997	Charlton	Home	3-1	Div 1
297	9/27/1997	Huddersfield	Home	1-1	Div 1
298/299	10/24/1997	Reading	Away	2-4	League Cup
300	2/19/1998	Bradford	Home	2-1	Div 1

Season 1998/99

301	8/15/1998	Oxford	Away	1-0	Div 1
302/303/304	8/18/1998	Barnet	Home	5-0	League Cup
305	8/28/1998	Watford	Away	2-0	Div 1
306	9/28/1998	Bury	Home	1-0	Div 1

(*Source: The Wolves' Site, www.thewolvessite.co.uk*)